WORK AT
HOME NOW

The No-Nonsense Guide to Finding
Your Perfect Home-Based Job, Avoiding
Scams, and Making a Great Living

By Christine Durst and
Michael Haaren

CAREER
PRESS

Franklin Lakes, NJ

WORK AT HOME NOW
EDITED BY JODI BRANDON
TYPESET BY DIANA GHAZZAWI
Cover design by Rob Johnson/Johnson Design
Printed in the U.S.A. by Courier

To order this title, please call toll-free 1-800-CAREER-1 (NJ and Canada: 201-848-0310) to order using VISA or MasterCard, or for further information on books from Career Press.

CAREER
PRESS

The Career Press, Inc., 3 Tice Road, PO Box 687,
Franklin Lakes, NJ 07417
www.careerpress.com

Library of Congress Cataloging-in-Publication Data

Durst, Christine, 1963–
    Work at home now : the no-nonsense guide to finding your perfect home-based job, avoiding scams, and making a great living / by Christine Durst and Michael Haaren.
        p. cm.
    Includes index.
    ISBN 978-1-60163-091-9
    1. Telecommuting--United States. 2. Home-based businesses--United States. I. Haaren, Michael, 1949– II.Title.

HD2336.35.U6D87 2010
658'.0412--dc22

                                                            2009036389

DEDICATION

To my parents, Ron and Bev Champany, for your constant love, guidance, and support. You taught me from a young age the importance of hard work, big dreams, and unshakable faith. Your lessons are with me always.

—Christine Champany Durst

To my wonderful children, Travis and Jazz. Some dads are lucky, but I'm the luckiest.

And to Ben and Betty Anne Fordney, who gave a teenager much-needed guidance.

—Michael Haaren

ACKNOWLEDGMENTS

First, we'd like to thank all the visitors to RatRaceRebellion.com and readers of the Rat Race Rebellion Telework Bulletin for supporting our work with your kudos, suggestions, and critiques. This book wouldn't exist without you. Also online, we'd like to thank the members of WorkPlaceLikeHome.com, WAHM.com, and other work-at-home communities who have shared warm and generous comments about us and our work.

To the many busy executives, home-based workers, and public relations representatives who took time from their days (and nights) to provide indispensable quotes and interviews for this book—our gratitude and appreciation.

The work-at-home movement would be crippled by scams if the media didn't alert consumers to the latest con games. We'd especially like to thank Jim Avila, Carla DeLandri, Ann Varney, and Ruth Reiss at ABC News *20/20*, and Don Lemon, Kyra Phillips, Randi Kaye, Glenn Emery, and Mykal Kristopher-Frierson at CNN for their work on exposing scammers, and giving us the opportunity to assist.

Telework is also indebted for innovation to the U.S. State Department's Family Liaison Office. Foreign Service families are fortunate to have you, as are we to work with you. On the Armed Forces side, we could fill whole books with good people, but for now would especially like to recognize Nancy Seckman, at Schriever Air Force Base's Airman & Family Readiness Center.

To our agent, Bob DiForio, go our thanks for invaluable support and effectiveness, and wise and patient counsel as the book came to life.

The team at Career Press has once again been a delight to work with, and we'd especially like to thank Michael Pye, Laurie Kelly-Pye, and Kirsten Dalley. Our line editor, Jodi Brandon (a writer in her own right), kept the egg off our faces repeatedly. Our gratitude to all.

Contents

Introduction

Almost every day by e-mail, and in our U.S. State Department and Armed Forces work-at-home workshops as well, people tell us they need to find a home-based job now:

> "I lost my job and want to replace it with a
> home-based job *now.*"

> "My commute is killing me and I need to work at home *now.*"

> "I need a home-based job *now,* that I can take with me
> when we move again."

> "My retirement nest egg vanished and I need a job *now.*"

> "I'm caring for a sick child and need a home-based job *now.*"

While writing this book, we focused on the "now" that job seekers have emphasized, to help you find the quickest route to home-based jobs and projects that meet your needs. You'll also find in-depth, action-ready details on more than 400 legitimate companies and other trustworthy sources of home-based work, rather than an introductory or overview approach.

Lastly, we've strived to avoid statistics-heavy discussions of telework studies (including our own), analytical treatments of business process outsourcing (BPO), and so forth. These are important, certainly, but aren't to the purpose here.

In short, we've tried to create the most practical guide we could, to help you find your best home-based job or project in the briefest possible time.

A word on our backgrounds

Chris likes to say that we know the work-at-home arena "better than most and as well as the rest," and, at the risk of sounding boastful, it's true. But bragging rights don't come without hard work in the right places. For us, these "right places" have included:

- ◆ **At the "magnifying glass,"** where every week we look at 4,500–5,000 work-at-home job listings and ads, to determine which are legitimate and which are scams.

- ◆ **In the media,** with CNN, ABC News *20/20*, *The Wall Street Journal*, *Consumers Digest*, *Woman's World*, and many more, where we expose scams and help people find authentic home-based work.

- ◆ **In our briefings** to the FBI, the Federal Trade Commission, the Department of Labor, and other agencies on the status of home-based jobs, scams, and telework.

- ◆ **At the podium,** in presentations to the President's Committee on Employment of People With Disabilities (home-based work is an important option for people with disabilities), the Presidential Task Force on Employment of Adults with Disabilities, the U.S Department of Labor's Workforce Innovations Conference, and many more.

- ◆ **In training rooms around the world,** where, in addition to programs for the State Department and Armed Forces, we and our certified trainers deliver virtual-career workshops to state agencies, colleges, faith-based organizations, nonprofit groups, and more.

- ◆ **Online,** on our popular RatRaceRebellion.com Website, in our virtual-careers column at Military.com, and in our telework bulletin, where we've helped people around the world make their work-at-home dreams a reality.

- ◆ **In *The 2-Second Commute*** (Career Press, 2005), our first book, which has guided thousands of people on the exciting new Virtual Assistant career path.

- ◆ *In our own home offices,* where between us we have more than 40 years' experience practicing what we preach.

Why we care about telework

When we addressed the United Nations on the subject of virtual work in 1999, we knew that the Internet held stunning promise to dramatically change the way we work and live.

Among other benefits, home-based work could significantly reduce our dependence on cars, enable parents to spend more time with their children, and foster "local living," too—imperative to offset global warming. (Coming from small towns in rural Connecticut and Virginia—Chris was raised on a farm, and Mike in a log cabin near the Blue Ridge Mountains—we have seen the beauty of "local living" in action.)

In putting homes ahead of cars, telework has the potential to repopulate "bedroom communities" by day, rescue the civic life that the rat race is stealing from us, boost local farming and commerce, reduce obesity, and help us get to know, and care about, one another again, the way we should.

Now, as virtual work finally begins to approach critical mass, we're delighted to arm you with the resources to join us among the happily, healthy, and gratefully home-based.

CHAPTER 1

Work-at-Home at a Glance

We said we wouldn't weigh you down with heavy statistics and other data about home-based work (and we won't), but we do want to share briefly some telework basics before we dig in to the good stuff. We promise to keep it short!

What is telework?

Telework has various definitions, but the simplest way to think of it might be "work that's done in an unconventional location, often from home, using electronic communications tools to send and receive workflow."

Though home-based telework will be our primary theme, telework takes many forms: a mom (or dad) handling customer-service calls in a spare room, a blogger writing in a café, a retiree answering questions on ChaCha.com from an RV park, a marketing exec videoconferencing back to company headquarters from a client's office—all are teleworking.

As wonderful as telework can be for the individual, remember that, from the employer's viewpoint, it's a management option rather than a worker right or "benefit," and is justified by the advantages it offers the company—not the worker. In the following pages, you'll hear companies say or imply this, and we'll repeat it, too, as it will help you optimize your resume and job applications, and start working ASAP.

While we're speaking of companies, historically they were reluctant (especially the larger Fortune 500s) to hire workers directly from home. Fortunately, companies such as Aetna, UnitedHealth Group, American Express, and others are moving away from the old customs, and hiring qualified workers to work from their homes immediately.

Categories of telework arrangements

Telework arrangements come in several categories: full, partial, and episodic or situational.

Full Telework is the situation many people seek. It involves working from home (or anywhere) 100 percent of the time, with perhaps an occasional trip to the company office, or in-office training before staying home. Many freelance workers or independent contractors (in other words, the self-employed) enjoy this arrangement.

Partial Telework usually consists of a regular schedule of one to three days per week at home, but can also include as few as two to three days per month. These schedules are often seen in corporate or federal/state agency telecommuting programs.

Situational or Episodic Telework has been getting more attention in what's called "business continuity," as companies see businesses shut down and lose revenues when man-made or natural disasters make office-based work impossible (for example, the 9/11 attacks, Hurricane Katrina, bird and swine flu, and so on).

Wildfires, earthquakes, and other disasters—as well as smaller events such as snowstorms and power outages—also make situational telework an attractive option for employers and workers alike.

Types of positions suited for telework

As you begin the search for home-based work, it's important to consider the types of positions or work employers are authorizing for telework. Studies as well as the job market itself indicate that these positions often involve workers who:

◆ Work alone or independently, with little or no supervision.

◆ Perform "knowledge-based" work rather than "production" tasks.

◆ Don't require daily or frequent face-to-face interaction with colleagues or managers.

◆ Don't need frequent access to on-site equipment and resources.

◆ Take the initiative, where appropriate, to make the arrangement work well for all concerned.

In the early days of telework, hirers often limited off-site arrangements to technical or other "analytic" work. As you'll see in the following chapters, those narrow boundaries have expanded greatly and are continuing to grow—creating home-based opportunities across a wide spectrum of jobs, and creating entirely new job categories as well.

Even so, the success of a telework arrangement depends as much on the nature of the worker as it does on the work, and not everyone is suited to be home-based. The self-assessment that follows in Chapter 2 will help you determine whether you're really ready to work at home.

Are You Ready to Work at Home?

In our years of delivering work-at-home training programs at the U.S. State Department, military bases, community colleges, and so on, we've found that successful teleworkers share certain traits which give them an advantage in a home-based position.

We've also met a fair number of people who, despite their genuine desire to work from home, wind up struggling when it becomes a reality.

The following self-assessment will help you determine whether you possess the traits that help home-based workers stay on track and succeed.

Read each of the numbered questions/statements and circle the answer that most accurately describes you or your situation. There are no right or wrong answers; the best approach is simply to be as honest as possible. Your candor will also help assure that the assessment results are accurate, which in turn will guide you toward changes you might make to improve your chances for telework success.

Work-at-home readiness assessment

1. **When it comes to socializing at work:**

   a. I need to socialize at work, and in fact I wouldn't have much of a social life at all if not for my interactions with coworkers.

   b. I consider my workplace my primary social outlet.

   c. I do what's necessary to be "accepted" at work, but I have a satisfying social life outside of work.

   d. I don't need constant interaction with my coworkers, and they often interrupt my workflow.

   e. I don't think people should socialize with their coworkers.

   f. I don't really care for other people very much.

2. **Do you organize projects or initiatives well, and get things done when they *should* be done?**

   a. No, never.

   b. Once in a while.

   c. Sometimes.

   d. More than half the time.

   e. Yes, most of the time.

   f. Always.

3. **How comfortable are you with the Internet?**

   a. I'm still using a typewriter and loving it!

   b. I don't know much about the Internet, and that's okay with me.

   c. I'm ready to spend more time on the Internet, but I'm not sure where to begin.

   d. I'm comfortable online, but I plan to have someone else handle online activities as soon as I can.

   e. I use the Internet regularly in my personal or work life.

   f. I've embraced the Internet entirely.

4. **Do you have trouble concentrating on tasks at hand because you're thinking of all the other things you have to do?**

a. All the time.

b. Frequently.

c. Quite a bit.

d. Sometimes.

e. Once in a while.

f. Not at all.

5. **How difficult do you find it to organize your activities so you can focus on and execute what's most important?**

   a. Things seem overwhelming most days.

   b. I try to plan, but somehow I get off track.

   c. I move ahead, but interruptions are a problem.

   d. I'm not a perfect organizer, but I manage to get everything done by putting in extra time.

   e. I'm a little disorganized, but by the end of my set hours I've accomplished everything necessary.

   f. Not at all.

6. **With regard to job-related goals:**

   a. I don't give them much value.

   b. I change my goals almost day to day.

   c. I've put nothing in writing, but know what I want to achieve.

   d. I set down my goals every January 1, but most are forgotten during the year.

   e. I've written out my goals, but some are probably far-fetched.

   f. I've listed goals that are specific, measurable, and realistic.

7. **When it comes to Internet- and computer-based business tools:**

   a. I swear by paper-based systems and have no plans to change.

   b. I love them for basic tasks such as word processing, but I've ventured no further.

   c. I understand they're a must and am making an effort to learn more.

    d.   I know how to use basic software programs and how to navigate the Internet fairly well.

    e.   I'm generally familiar with them but rely mainly on the expertise of others.

    f.   I'm comfortable with them and look forward to learning more.

8.   **How often do you answer e-mail tardily, neglect to return a call, miss a deadline, or otherwise fall short from juggling too many things at once?**

    a.   All the time.

    b.   Very often.

    c.   Quite a bit.

    d.   Not frequently, but enough to bother me.

    e.   Once in a great while.

    f.   Never.

9.   **A friend calls during a workday to tell you about a great one-day sale at your favorite store. You:**

    a.   Tell yourself "a sale is a sale!" and drop everything to go shopping.

    b.   Skim through your work so you can get to the store before the sale is over.

    c.   Tell her you'll only be able to take a three-hour break, and go.

    d.   Compose and e-mail her a list of things you want her to pick up for you at the sale.

    e.   Take five minutes to treat yourself to one or two things at the store's Website.

    f.   Beg off, and go back to work.

10.   **How supportive will your family and/or housemates be of your working from home?**

    a.   100 percent.

    b.   Very much.

    c.   Quite a bit.

    d.   Some.

    e.   Very little.

    f.   Not at all.

11. **In general, would you say you are equally able to lead and to follow?**

   a. Not at all.

   b. Once in a while.

   c. Sometimes.

   d. More than half the time.

   e. Most of the time.

   f. Always.

12. **If you work from home, will you be able to make time for exercise, family and friends, and just plain fun?**

   a. Yes, as much as I need to.

   b. Yes, most of the time.

   c. Probably more than half the time.

   d. Sometimes.

   e. Once in a while.

   f. No, never.

13. **Which of the following most closely describes your communication tools?**

   a. Phone and mail only.

   b. Phone, fax, and mail.

   c. Phone, fax, mail, and e-mail.

   d. Phone, fax, mail, e-mail, and instant messenger.

   e. Phone, fax, mail, e-mail, instant messenger, e-mail lists, and Internet message boards.

   f. All of the above, and some you didn't mention!

14. **Are you an effective communicator, stating your wishes clearly, listening well, and checking for the need for clarification?**

   a. Always.

   b. Most of the time.

   c. More than half the time.

   d. Sometimes.

   e. Once in a while.

   f. No, never.

15. **When you have technical difficulties with your computer, can you troubleshoot the problem and fix it yourself?**

    a. Yes, always.

    b. Yes, most of the time.

    c. More than half the time.

    d. Sometimes.

    e. Once in a while.

    f. No, never.

16. **Does your family disregard your "personal space," and use, misplace, or break things that belong to you?**

    a. All the time.

    b. Very often.

    c. Quite a bit.

    d. Sometimes.

    e. Rarely.

    f. Not at all.

17. **Do you look forward to teleworking because you'll be able to wear sweat clothes all day, run errands when you want, and not have the stress of a real work environment?**

    a. Extremely so.

    b. Very much.

    c. Quite a bit.

    d. Somewhat.

    e. A little.

    f. Not at all.

18. **When you set out to complete an important task, does it get done, no matter how boring or distasteful you may find it?**

    a. Never.

    b. Rarely.

    c. Occasionally.

    d. Usually.

    e.   Frequently.

    f.   Always.

19.   Is there an area or room in your home where you can set up a workspace and be free from noise and distractions?

    a.   Yes.

    b.   There soon will be, with little effort.

    c.   There could be, once I get organized.

    d.   It will take an awful lot of work.

    e.   It's almost impossible.

    f.   No.

20.   Will your working space be secure, and protected against unauthorized access?

    a.   Yes, no one will have access without my permission.

    b.   Only my spouse or significant other will have access.

    c.   It isn't secure now, but I can make it so.

    d.   It would take an awful lot of work.

    e.   It's almost impossible.

    f.   No.

Scoring your assessment

To score your assessment, go to the grid that follows and simply match the number of the question (in the dark column on the left, with numbers 1 through 20) and the letter that corresponds to your answer (in the columns headed a–f).

Your score for each question will be the number in the square where the question row and the answer column intersect. For example, if your answer to question number 2 is e, your score would be 4.

For each question, write your score in the non-shaded square in the Assessment Areas columns, headed TT, TM, EQ, and TQ.

When you've listed all of your scores in the appropriate Assessment Areas columns, tally the numbers in each of the columns and enter your totals on the bottom row.

	a.	b.	c.	d.	e.	f.		TT	TM	EQ	TQ
1.	0	2	5	4	1	0	►				
2.	0	1	2	3	4	5	►				
3.	0	1	2	3	4	5	►				
4.	0	1	2	3	4	5	►				
5.	0	1	2	3	4	5	►				
6.	0	1	2	3	4	5	►				
7.	0	1	2	3	4	5	►				
8.	0	1	2	3	4	5	►				
9.	0	1	1	2	3	5	►				
10.	5	4	3	2	1	0	►				
11.	0	1	2	3	4	5	►				
12.	5	4	3	2	1	0	►				
13.	0	1	2	3	4	5	►				
14.	5	4	3	2	1	0	►				
15.	5	4	3	2	1	0	►				
16.	0	1	2	3	4	5	►				
17.	0	1	2	3	4	5	►				

Assessment Areas

	a.	b.	c.	d.	e.	f.		TT	TM	EQ	TQ
								Assessment Areas			
18.	0	1	2	3	4	5	►				
19.	5	4	3	2	1	0	►				
20.	5	4	3	2	1	0	►				
	Totals for Each Area:										

Interpreting your scores

The self-assessment questions were developed to help you identify certain traits and characteristics that could have an impact—positive or negative—on your success as a home-based worker.

Your score in each of the four Assessment Areas columns reveals your self-perceived profile in four key areas, and provides you with the following measurements:

TT = Telework Traits Quotient (highest possible score is 35)

Your Telework Traits Quotient relates to attitudes, traits, and characteristics that are at the center of successful telework relationships.

Score	
26–35	A score in this range suggests you possess many of the traits and characteristics most commonly found in successful teleworkers. You respect and value this work arrangement and are prepared to do what you must to make it succeed for you and your employer or client.

15–25	A score in this range suggests you have several of the core characteristics most commonly found in successful teleworkers, but some areas may prove troublesome.
	Reassess your answers. Will you struggle with the solitude of telework? Will you have the discipline to complete your work despite distractions?
	Make a plan to work through the possible issues before you take on a telework position. Then start with a limited telework arrangement—perhaps one or two days a week—and move gradually toward more days at home, as (or if) you adjust to your new work environment.
Less than 15	A score in this range suggests you may not be fully prepared for a telework arrangement. Your work style and preferences may make it difficult for you to manage work in a nontraditional environment.
	Though you see the benefits of working from home, you may perceive yourself as someone who doesn't possess a high level of self-discipline.
	We'd recommend that you work on honing your self-management skills before you seek a telework job.
	If you're currently employed, ask your manager if you can work from home once or twice a month, and see how you fare on those days. Track your successes and failures so you can continue the former and find solutions for the latter.
Resources for improving your Telework Traits Quotient	Recommended reading: *100 Ways to Motivate Yourself* by Steve Chandler *Motivation and Goal-Setting* by Jim Cairo *Deliberate Success: Realize Your Vision with Purpose, Passion and Performance* by Eric Allenbaugh

TM = Time Management Quotient
(highest possible score is 25)

Your Time Management Quotient relates to the demands on your time, how much control you feel you have over how your time is spent, how you manage multiple priorities and interruptions, and your ability to stay on track.

Score	
21–25	A score in this range suggests you are extremely skilled at orchestrating your day and staying focused on the most important activities. It's likely you're adept at handling the unexpected, and you resist the temptation to overbook your days. Your excellent time-management skills should help you find success as a home-based worker.
12–20	Individuals scoring in this range often find it hard to steer clear of unexpected events and interruptions. As a result, they may suffer from the imbalance that comes with always having to catch up on both business and personal matters. Developing your time-management skills before taking on telework could help you find greater satisfaction and success in a home-based role.
Less than 12	A score in this range suggests you are walking a time tightrope, and struggle with prioritizing the tasks at hand. The demands of work may already interfere with your personal and family time. You're likely to be overstressed in your work and home environments, and to feel that time controls you rather than vice versa. Reassess the way you manage your time, and invest in a good time-management course or book before considering a move to telework. Failure to manage your time well in a home-based work environment can lead to near-toxic stress.

Resources for improving your Time Management Quotient	Recommended reading: *Time Management In an Instant: 60 Ways to Make the Most of Your Day* by Karen Leland and Keith Bailey *151 Quick Ideas to Manage Your Time* by Robert E. Dittmer *Get Organized* by Ronald W. Fry Websites: Visit *www.mindtools.com* for time-management tips and a free newsletter.

EQ = Environmental Quotient
(highest possible score is 20)

Your Environmental Quotient reflects how conducive your home environment will be to effective and productive work. Your score takes into account your physical surroundings as well as the attitudes of those with whom you share your home.

Score	
11–20	A score in this range suggests you have a well-settled home that will provide the quiet and protected setting you'll need to work effectively. You feel that family members or others in your home will understand the need to respect your time, equipment, and space. This should be an ideal environment for teleworking.
5–10	A score in this range suggests that minor improvements may be needed before you undertake a home-based position. Preliminary steps toward a sound and secure work environment will increase your chances of success in a telework job.

| Less than 5 | A score in this range suggests you may not be able to provide an ideal environment for home-based work. If the environment is busy or noisy and others are likely to interrupt your work, you may succumb to the chaos, and lose the focus and momentum that tasks demand. Security may also be an issue for you. Depending upon your specific issues and the type of telework you seek, perhaps you can work from another location, such as a coworking or telework center. |
| *Resources for improving your Environmental Quotient* | <u>Recommended reading</u>: *Stop Clutter From Stealing Your Life* by Mike Nelson |

TQ = Technology Quotient (highest possible score is 20)

Your Technology Quotient is essentially a pulse check on your current comfort level with the Internet and related technology.

Telework is almost always a technology-enabled work arrangement. Therefore, it's important that you be comfortable with current technology, or at minimum have the capability, desire, and opportunity to learn about new programs and tools.

Score	
11–20	You're riding the crest of the wave into the networked economy. By maintaining a high level of knowledge, and willingness to try new things, you're well-positioned for success as a teleworker.

5–10	A score in this range suggests you've recognized the Internet as a valuable tool, and you're prepared to take steps to use it effectively in your work. However, you may also feel that your expertise isn't as strong as it could be, and you may occasionally fall back onto old systems when things pile up. You may want to take a class, do some background reading, or just spend more hands-on time with your computer to beef up your skills and comfort level.
Less than 5	People scoring in this range often report that their computer serves as nothing more than a glorified typewriter. Because teleworking is largely a technology-enabled way of working, it's important that you take the time and initiative to upgrade your skills. Be brave! Get online as soon as you can, and start exploring the environment that holds the keys to your future success.
Resources for improving your Technology Quotient	Websites: About.com netforbeginners.about.com/

With apologies to Shakespeare, readiness isn't all

If you're sure you've got the right stuff to work from home, that's wonderful, and we're here to help you do exactly that. Even so, it's critical to be realistic when you're considering making home your worksite. Be sure to weigh the potential drawbacks as well as the pluses. You can be "ready" to work from home, but still not *suited* to work from home.

Most of us are familiar with the advantages of home-based work, but let's recap them briefly in case there are a few you haven't considered.

Potential pros include:

1.   Lower stress levels.

Assuming, of course, that your home isn't stressful, you'll take a big step toward a healthier lifestyle by just leaving the car parked. Commuting has been linked to high blood pressure, insomnia, back problems, obesity, and other ills (not to mention accidents and road rage), so the sooner you can get out of the auto, the better off you'll be.

2. A chance to make it to that Little League game.

Depending on your hours (some home-based workers go overboard, as we mention in #5 of the cons against home-based work) and the type of work you do, working from home can give you the flexibility for better work/family balance.

Many home-based workers find it easier to get a child to that dental appointment or finally to be included in family meals. Bedtime stories, Little League games, and even volunteering to read to your child's school class (co-author Mike often does this, and Chris chaperoned field trips and baked treats for their classes when her children were small) can all suddenly become feasible when work and home are blended.

3. Reduced work-related expenses.

Most people never calculate their "cost of working"— the out-of-pocket expenses directly related to their job. When they do, it may suddenly answer the question: "Where does all my money go?"

We encourage you to calculate your own cost of brick-and-mortar work per month, and see how much it might save you to work at home. Be sure to include:

◆ Transportation expenses: gas, tolls, parking, auto maintenance and wear-and-tear, and insurance (and/or bus, cab, train fares, if these apply).

◆ Office wardrobe expenses: clothing purchases, alteration costs, and dry-cleaning charges.

◆ Lunch expenses: costs beyond what you would pay for lunch at home.

◆ Office "chip-in" expenses: all of those cards, cakes, meals, and coworker gifts that on-site workers often pay for.

◆ Dinner expenses: meals you eat out or buy on your way home.

◆   Miscellaneous work-related expenses.

◆   Childcare expenses. Can you reduce these by
     working from home?

4.   No commute = more time.

Assuming you commute, say, 45 minutes per day, five
days per week, that's 3.75 hours traveling to and from work
each week. Multiply that by 48 weeks (allowing for two weeks'
vacation and 10 holidays/sick days per year), and you're
spending 180 hours a year shuttling back and forth for the
cube. That's 22.5 eight-hour days—with no pay!

As a teleworker, you'll surely find something better to do
with that time.

5.   More control over your work environment.

If you've ever had to work next to a gum-popper, a gossip, a complainer, or any of the other endearing personalities
so often encountered in the workplace, you'll appreciate your
newfound authority over your work setting.

In your home office, you have the power to decide what
the temperature will be, whether there will be music (and if
so, what kind), and what, if anything, you will wear. In other
words, you are finally in charge, and can construct the work
environment that suits you best.

6.   Greater productivity.

Naturally, this "pro" depends largely on whom you share
your home with, and how well they stick to any ground rules
you set regarding your work space and your time. However,
studies routinely show that home-based workers are more
productive than their cube-bound counterparts, often as
much as 30 percent or more.

It's not hard to see why. In traditional offices, interruptions can be chronic and harder to control than at home,
and the "cubicle drive-by" committed by the chatty coworker
has become a fact of daily life. Home-based workers are also
often grateful for their convenient situation, and work harder
to keep it. And finally, not all workers are most productive
during the usual nine-to-five, and find that telework lets them
achieve peak performance during unconventional hours,
when they work best.

7. A wider choice of jobs, at higher pay.

   A traditional job search must usually be limited to a certain radius of your home. If local employment is flat, or confined to a narrow range of skills, your options are hobbled, too. Salaries or wages may be similarly restricted. With telework, technology leapfrogs the distance, and you can pursue jobs or projects that may originate hundreds or thousands of miles away, with higher compensation and more interesting work.

Potential cons include:

1. Home and community life can spill into work.

   Household chores, "needy" family members, and even the TV can be hard to ignore when you're working from home. (And how about bored cats walking on keyboards, or loud children in apartment hallways?) Spouses or friends can also require firm and repeated instruction before they really understand that "home-based" doesn't mean "available for errands or chit-chat."

2. Absence of peers or bosses can lead to slackness.

   For many teleworkers, the physical absence of a boss and coworkers can be a double-edged sword. Although they won't be interrupting you as often, they won't be nearby to create the pressure you might need to perform effectively, or kindle your competitive fires.

   Working "away" from the team, you'll need serious self-discipline to maintain a good work ethic.

3. Feelings of loneliness and isolation, and a loss of morale.

   Most of us are herd animals, and teleworkers often acutely miss the elbow-to-elbow side of conventional office life. Plus, where's that pat on the back when you've done a good job? (Somehow, an e-mail isn't quite the same.) Morale, job satisfaction, and performance are all up for grabs if you're not suited to the solitude that telework can sometimes bring.

4. No escape from either "work" or "home."

   When you commute, the office can be an escape from pressures at home, and leaving the office building at day's end usually means leaving "work" behind, too. But when your office is in your home, you've just lost both exits. Teleworkers must create and maintain new habits and structures to keep healthy divisions between home and work.

5. Working too many hours.

In the same vein, with the ebb and flow and cues and signals of the conventional office day gone—and the computer always only a step away—teleworkers run the risk of overwork, and disrupted family time—as in, "I need to check my e-mail, but I'll be back in five minutes!" Two hours later, the chair at the dinner table is still empty.

6. "Out of sight, out of mind."

In an office environment, the boss gets the impact and payoff of seeing you at your desk, working hard and pulling those extra hours. In other words, there's a tangible demonstration of your commitment, team spirit, and work ethic.

Likewise, your boss and colleagues may have little or no face time with you, and your quick smile, cheery disposition, charm, scintillating wit, bottomless fund of knock-knock jokes, and so forth, will all go off their radar. Similarly, you won't be handy for those informal (and rapport-building) chats with your boss, and may not be privy to the critical "back channel" information that's so often shared by co-workers in the office.

In other words, off-site workers are more likely than their commuting colleagues to be judged solely on the quality and/or quantity of their work. And when promotion time comes around, you may be out of mind as well as out of sight. (In other words—as we'll often repeat—full-time telework, with home in one place and "headquarters" distant, isn't for everyone.)

But don't let either the pros or the cons unduly sway you. If you're ready and well-suited to work from home, the odds of success and satisfaction will be with you. And if you sincerely want to work from home but need to make adjustments, then by all means move ahead. Perhaps you'll have to learn new skills, or develop a social circle outside the office. Maybe the children will require some new rules, or you'll have to dig down a bit for self-discipline and some new habits.

Making home your work base may mean having to change a lot of things. But in the end, it may well turn out to be one of the most rewarding personal, family, and career choices you've ever made.

CHAPTER 3

Convincing Your Boss to Let You Work From Home

If you're already employed doing something you love—but you'd also love to eliminate or reduce your commute—then this chapter is for you.

But first, we'll take a moment to repeat an important point we noted in the first chapter: Until the law deems otherwise, *telework is a management option rather than an employee right or "benefit," and is justified by the advantages it offers the company—not the employee.*

In other words, until environmental or other imperatives create a right to telework, companies will evaluate telework proposals not as service requests, but as they would any other business proposition. In other words: *What's in it for me?*

Accordingly, if you plan to broach the topic of telework with your boss, keep his or her company perspective in mind at all times: *What's in it for me?* Doing so can mean the difference between hearing "We don't do that here" and "Okay, let's give it a try, and see how you do."

And to get to that "yes" point, you'll want to present a well-considered case for why having you work from home is the right decision for the company.

Have a plan, not a request

Throughout the years, many people have told us that they've asked bosses and supervisors if they could work from home, only to be rejected outright. When we ask how they approached the topic, far too often the reply is that "I just told him that I need to be at home with my kids."

As compassionate people and parents ourselves, we can sympathize with the employee's—and children's—needs. (After all, one of the prime reasons we launched our home-based jobs Website, RatRaceRebellion.com, was to help parents and children spend more time together.) But as business owners, too, we can also see why the bosses said no.

In most cases, the manager is probably sympathetic to the employee's plight, but the harsh truth is that childcare issues (or an aging parent, an outrageous commute, unreliable transportation, and so forth) are not his or her problem, and solving it is not perceived as a source of profit to the company. The manager—and his or her boss all the way up to the board room—has a list of goals for a given reporting period, and "helping Employee X spend more time with her children" usually isn't on it.

Indeed, though it may sound cold, if a company starts making decisions based on feelings instead of earnings, profits may suffer, and jobs may be put at risk—including yours.

So let's explore how you can wow the boss with a company-oriented plan, instead of a self-oriented request.

Creating a winning telework proposal

Here, we'll walk you through a step-by-step process for creating a winning proposal. Those steps will include:

1. Drafting an attention-grabbing opening statement.
2. Outlining the benefits to the company.
3. Breaking down your daily tasks and commitments.
4. Proposing a schedule and highlighting your flexibility.
5. Suggesting methods for quantifying your productivity.
6. Reminding your boss what a valuable asset you are to the company.
7. Describing your home-based workspace and equipment.

1. Drafting an attention-grabbing opening statement

Length: 1 to 3 paragraphs

Open your proposal with a short statement that will make your boss want to read more. (Though this section will appear first, you'll want to write it last, so you can weave in supporting statistics and other data you find in your research.)

Here's an example:

Mr. Boss,

Now more than ever, corporations large and small are embracing tele-work, and letting employees periodically work from home. Many factors are driving the movement, including increased employee productivity and decreased turnover, business-continuity concerns, rising real estate and fuel costs, and the company's environmental image.

Some companies, like Best Buy, have gone even further, significantly boosting productivity and reducing turnover by adopting a "Results-Only Work Environment" (ROWE), permitting employees—including managers— to work from anywhere as long as they achieve their targets.

I have assessed my duties here at Widget, Inc., and, as this telework proposal will show, I believe I can be an even greater asset to the company if I am permitted to work periodically at home. Indeed, a "time and task" audit that I recently completed of my in-office work revealed that eliminating "drop-in" interruptions alone could result in 15% more productivity on days when I am working at home.

I will look forward to discussing this proposal with you, and exploring how a trial telework period might demonstrate substantial benefits for our team and a positive impact on the company's bottom line.

Respectfully,

Ms. Teleworker

2. Outlining the benefits to the company

Length: 2 pages

We usually refer to this as the "What's in it for them?" section of the proposal ("them" being your employer, of course). Here, you'll show in detail how you've considered a telework arrangement from the employer's viewpoint, and you'll lay out the compelling reasons why it would directly benefit the company.

This is often the "make or break" part of a proposal. Be prepared to roll up your sleeves and spend plenty of time searching for facts and statistics that will "hit home," so to speak, with your boss.

Using the following chart, and thinking specifically about what motivates your company and its managers, outline what you *assume* the benefits of a telework arrangement will be to the business. We've listed several "action words" and benefits as thought starters, and additional lines for you to use to round out the list with others that fit your own unique situation.

Note: *For more ideas, consider the buzz words and phrases that recur in company meetings and memos, and conversations with your boss. These can be good indicators of what's on management's mind.*

Through adoption of the proposed telework arrangement, the company will:	
Save	time, money
Increase	revenues, customer satisfaction*, customer loyalty*
Improve	productivity, morale, recruitment, and the quality of its workforce
Reduce	expenses, sick time, absenteeism
Promote	a family-friendly image, a "green" public image or business practice

*These benefits are often reported by call centers, for example, with home-based agents.

Now, with your list as a reference point, you can begin the research that will back up your *assumptions* with hard facts! Ideally, you'll want to gather meaningful statistics from respected studies and industry reports.

With these goals in mind, start your research with your favorite search engine. Use search terms that include the *form* of the information you're seeking (*statistics, findings, research, studies,* and so on) "+" the assumption you are hoping to support (for example, "telework saves time").

For example, using the action words *save* and *increase* that we listed in the chart, your search terms (which would not be enclosed in quotation marks, because you're searching for concepts rather than exact phrases) might include:

◆ statistics + telework saves time

◆ studies + telework saves time

◆ findings + telework saves time

◆ research + telework saves time

◆ statistics + telework saves money

◆ studies + telework saves money

◆ findings + telework saves money

◆ research + telework saves money

◆ statistics + telework increases income

◆ studies + telework increases income

◆ findings + telework increases income

◆ research+ telework increases income

◆ statistics + telework increases customer satisfaction

◆ studies + telework increases customer satisfaction

◆ findings + telework increases customer satisfaction

◆ research + telework increases customer satisfaction

Hint: To find additional data, try these searches using "telecommute" or "telecommuting" in the place of "telework."

In reviewing your search results, give the greatest weight to information found on sites with a solid reputation in the telework arena, or that your boss will otherwise consider reliable. Examples of respected telework resource sites include, but are not limited to:

◆ InnoVisions Canada: ivc.ca (both Canadian and non-Canadian information).

◆ Telework Coalition: telcoa.org.

◆ Telework Advisory Group: workingfromanywhere.org.

◆ Telework Exchange: teleworkexchange.com.

◆ Telecommute Connecticut: telecommutect.com.

◆ Commuter Challenge: commuterchallenge.org.

◆ Network World: networkworld.com (search the site for "telecommuting").

◆ Euro-Telework: euro-telework.org.

◆ JALA International: jala.com.

◆ Telework.gov, and other federal government telework sites.

◆ Various college/university telework research sites.

◆ State government telework sites.

◆ Newspaper and magazine sites reporting on telework.

To strengthen your case for working from home, do some research to see whether your company's competitors—or firms it simply respects or would like to emulate—have telework programs, and cite their successes. For example, if your company competes with Sun Microsystems, simply Google "Sun Microsystems" + telecommuting, and you'll find data on the success of Sun's telework program to bolster your proposal.

Now, compile your most compelling findings in an easy-to-skim format (most managers don't have the time to read a heavy narrative-style document). A bullet-point list usually works best, but if you have a knack for organizing data in another format (and you'll know your boss's preferences, too), by all means do so.

3. Breaking down your daily tasks and commitments

Length: 2 to 3 pages, depending on your job description

This section of your proposal is the "reality check"—an assessment of whether your job can actually be done from home.

To show your boss you've given this proposal due thought, you'll need to analyze every aspect of your job—the tasks you manage, who you interact with, what resources you use, how you deliver your work, and so on—and explain which duties you can do from home, and how.

If your company uses written job descriptions, these may be a good starting place. However, as most employees will attest, it's a rare description that captures a job's every facet. Therefore, we suggest conducting a "time and task audit," in which you record during a one-week period (or two to three days, if your job is repetitive) everything you *really* do. Though this can be tedious and takes time, the data can reinforce your proposal substantially.

To get started on the audit, create an audit worksheet with the following column headers: time, activity, home, office, and "AI" (avoidable interruptions). Separate your typical workday into 10-minute increments. (The following example shows the first few hours of a workday that begins at 8:00 a.m.) This can be done by hand, if you prefer, but your word processor or spreadsheet application will create a clean form that can be printed out or completed on your computer.

Now you're ready to conduct your audit. Throughout the course of your workday:

1. In the "Activity" column, briefly note the task you were involved in during the time specified on the left.
2. If the activity could be done as well or better from home, place an "X" in the "Home" column. If better done in the office, place an "X" in the "Office" column.
3. Each time your activities are interrupted for non-productive reasons, place an "X" in the "AI" column.

Time	Activity	Home	Office	AI
08:00	Check and reply to e-mail	X		
:10	Herb—talking about *Survivor*			X
:20	Sherry stopped to discuss the Abbott account	X		
:30	Check and reply to e-mail	X		
:40	Check and reply to e-mail	X		
:50	Check and reply to e-mail	X		
09:00	Call to XYZ, Inc. re: monthly re-order	X		
:10	Call to XYZ, Inc. re: monthly re-order	X		
:20	Herb—money for Bob's birthday; *American Idol*			X
:30	Draft proposal for ABC, Inc.	X		
:40	X			
:50	X			
10:00	Sales meeting		X	
:10	Sales meeting		X	

:20	Sales meeting		X	
:30	Sales meeting		X	
:40	Sales meeting		X	
:50	Sales meeting		X	
11:00	Herb—"How was the meeting?"			X
:10	Sherry—"I just heard about the meeting…"			X
:20	Back to ABC, Inc. proposal	X		

At the end of your audit period, you'll have a snapshot of your typical workweek, and an accurate idea of how much of your work you can do from home.

You'll also have another important detail: the amount of time you are unproductive each day due to interruptions that could have been avoided if you had been at home—your AIs. (Needless to add, this assumes you'll take every reasonable measure to fend off the AIs that can beset you in a home office!)

Armed with your audit, you can present your boss with a comprehensive overview of your duties, the percentage of work you can perform from home, and the productive time you'll gain by relocating yourself to a setting more conducive to uninterrupted work.

4. Proposing a schedule and highlighting your flexibility

Length: 2 to 3 paragraphs

The key to an acceptable telework schedule ("acceptable" as defined primarily by management, of course) is to transition into the arrangement conservatively, at a pace your boss can be comfortable with. (If you perform well, the schedule you yourself would prefer will hopefully follow.) Although aggressive schedules are easy for management to refuse, a well-planned "trial period" might seem not only eminently reasonable, but even an exciting experiment—one that could spearhead a larger telework program within the company.

A preliminary schedule of just one or two days per week can often work well, weighted toward the days that would work best for your boss and colleagues. In this early phase, you might want to avoid requesting telework days on Mondays or Fridays, as coworkers may decide that you've finagled a "long weekend" setup, while they're stuck back at the office. And among other side effects, their sour grapes won't help your cause when it comes time to petition the company to make the trial arrangement permanent.

Regardless of the schedule you propose, be sure your boss knows you're willing to be flexible. Some managers, regardless of how well-weighed the plan, will want to tweak it a bit to make it their own. Now is the time to give a little, and show you're a team player.

Remember: Even if the boss concedes to only one telework day per week, this still gives you the opening to demonstrate the superb value of that day to the company, and the multiple value of more.

5. Suggesting methods for quantifying your productivity

Length: 1 page

It's important to remember that most managers have never supervised a remote workforce, and you may be asking yours to take a step outside his or her managerial comfort zone. Regardless, managers often note (or by stonewalling even minimal telework initiatives, betray) their concern that employees will be unproductive if unwatched. In this section of your proposal, you can ease any such concerns by suggesting ways in which your productivity can be measured.

As an example, you might:

- ◆ Provide your boss with a list of measurable goals, against which he or she can gauge your performance.

- ◆ Suggest applications such as Norton PCAnywhere or Citrix GoToMyPC to enable you to work on your office computer from your home computer. This will permit your boss to monitor your activities simply by looking at your in-office computer screen.

- ◆ Agree to e-mail a report at the end of each day, summarizing activities and outcomes.

- ◆ Make yourself available by instant messenger during business hours.

- ◆ Commit to check messages and return phone calls within a certain time.

◆   Set a schedule for phone check-ins.

◆   Make it known that you can be at the main office within a certain time if urgent situations arise.

◆   Set up a pager or other backup communication methods your boss can rely on in the event normal systems fail.

As you, your boss, and your colleagues adapt to your home-based work arrangement, you may find that your boss doesn't require the reassuring touches he preferred in the beginning. But regardless, the more pains you take to make the trial period transparent, the more likely you'll be moving toward a permanent and liberal telework schedule.

6. Reminding your boss what a valuable asset you are to the company

Length: 1 page

Making a case for "you" as a viable work-at-home candidate is an important step in sealing your telework deal. (Indeed, it helps to approach the entire campaign as if you were applying for a job.) After all, it would be a pity to persuade the boss to embrace the idea of telework—but not for you! Use this section of your proposal to strut your stuff, and remind your boss of all the wonderful attributes and accomplishments that make you the ideal candidate for off-site work.

If written performance evaluations pertinently sing your praises, be sure to quote them often in your proposal. The goal is to get your boss to focus on the traits that ideal teleworkers also share. For example, you want your boss to know that you are:

◆   A self-starter.

◆   An excellent organizer of time, tasks, and priorities.

◆   An independent problem-solver.

◆   A solid team player.

◆   Self-disciplined.

◆   Self-directed.

◆   Technically savvy and able to manage basic troubleshooting.

◆   An excellent communicator.

Naturally, your list will need supporting evidence, with clear examples of accomplishments and contributions that demonstrate your ideal teleworker qualities.

7. Describing your home-based workspace and equipment

Length: 1 page

It may sound mundane, but it's important to paint a picture of your work environment for your boss. This will not only help him or her visualize you working there, but also show that the space is professional-grade and free of distractions. Ideally, your proposal will include photographs of your home-based workspace, but you can make do with a diagram and a written description.

To help make the sale, you might also consider inviting your boss to your home office before the telework arrangement begins, and smooth the way thereafter with scheduled visits when you are working from home. (Again, as his or her comfort level increases, your boss may find this reassurance unnecessary.)

In your office description, be sure to include details that show you've given due consideration to security and safety issues. For example:

◆ The home office is free from excessive noise.

◆ The wiring will accommodate a computer and other office equipment, and surge protectors are in place.

◆ The desk and chair are ergonomically correct, and there is excellent lighting in the work area.

◆ The computer is connected to a battery backup/surge protector to ensure no data loss in case of a power loss or surge.

◆ The office is well ventilated and has an exit in case of emergency.

◆ The office is equipped with smoke detectors and a fire extinguisher.

◆ The office is in a secure area where no one, including family members, will have access to work equipment or data.

Be sure to address any unique or extraordinary concerns your company might have about the confidentiality of information and system security. Similarly, if telework will require the company to provide equipment for your home office, address those issues here.

Other points to consider include:

◆ Will you need a fax machine, an additional phone line, or an external hard drive?

◆ How will you handle backing up your system?

◆ Will the company provide insurance to cover any loss of equipment or data from the home office?

Finally, diffuse any concerns there might be about your personal life encroaching on your work at home. For example, tell your boss up front what childcare or eldercare arrangements you've made for your telework days. Note that your loyal Mastiff or beloved Macaw will be kept beyond sound's reach, and won't disturb you or be heard by colleagues and clients on the phone.

Anticipating questions such as these in your proposal and solving them wherever possible will reassure your boss and improve your chances of a green light.

Be prepared to talk about your proposal

Don't sit back and let your proposal do the talking. You should be as prepared to state your case live as you have in writing. Take the time to anticipate any oral questions your boss might have, and be ready to address them.

You probably know your boss well, and have a sense of what he or she will want to cover in person. Perhaps as you write your proposal, you'll hear his or her voice in your head—questioning facts or assertions, or wondering how certain aspects of the arrangement will work. Your ability to answer questions with confidence and clarity will strengthen the likelihood of the "yes" you're hoping for.

Even so, the fates may intervene. If the thumb turns down, remember the points your boss had a hard time getting past, and take steps to help him or her overcome those obstacles. For example, if you have an opportunity to work at home to finish up a project after hours or over a weekend, take it. In business, nothing speaks as loudly as results, and you may soon give your boss reason to reflect on the error of his or her ways.

CHAPTER 4

Developing Your "BS" (Big Scam) Radar

The demand for home-based work has always been strong. (Even George and Martha Washington worked from home.) But when jobs generally are scarce, and as the rat race grows ever more stressful, the demand surges. Unfortunately, scammers track trends even better than most economists do, and when they see the demand—for anything—outpacing the supply, they rush to bilk consumers out of their hard-earned cash.

To the scamming community, the demand for home-based work is akin to someone shouting, "There's gold in those hills!" in a Gold Rush. And make no mistake, there is a scamming community—complete with online forums where con artists gather to applaud each other's efforts, and share their best tips for ripping you off.

On one such forum, we found a thread dedicated to how to draw people into work-at-home scams. The advice that was dispensed—scammer-to-scammer—included:

◆ Post a "vague, but intriguing" ad to the craigslist job section.

◆ Structure the listing so it "looks like a legit job."

◆ "Make up a name" for job seekers to reply to.

◆ Set up an auto-responder message to tell applicants—regardless of their qualifications—that their application has been reviewed, and they are a "perfect fit for our company."

◆ Direct job seekers to a Website and tell them to complete an online form, which serves as a "capture page" (scammers use "capture pages" to obtain personal information).

◆ Set up a "drip campaign" of messages to "weed out the garbage," and produce a reliable list of prospective victims.

As you can see, scammers plan their cons very carefully. They take the time to set perfect traps for the prey they're stalking, set with juicy, succulent bait. Many scammers could make a living as honest businesspeople if they wanted to, for they're smart, tenacious, and exceptionally imaginative.

And believe us, we've met (and peered into) work-at-home scams of every shape and size. Professionally, we've briefed the FBI and the Federal Trade Commission on scams (as we write, we're working with them on a scam that has victimized tens of thousands of people internationally), and Chris reports regularly on scams on CNN and other media. We review between 4,500 and 5,000 work-at-home job leads every week, publishing the legitimate leads to our RatRaceRebellion.com Website and our biweekly telework bulletin.

We've encountered crude scams, to be sure, but many are diabolically well-disguised, with Websites (usually here today, gone tomorrow) that pull in millions of prospective victims every month.

The rising "scam ratio"

As part of our screening process, we track what we refer to as the "scam ratio": the number of scam job leads we see in the marketplace compared to the number of legitimate leads. And the ratio has been worsening rapidly.

The statistics tell the story. In February 2006, for example, the scam ratio was 30 to 1, meaning that for every 31 jobs we researched, only one was legitimate. By October of the same year, the ratio had soared to 42-to-1—a whopping *40-percent increase*. And it has continued to rise. As we write, the scam ratio hovers between 55 to 1 and 59 to 1.

Given the tough job market, the need for beefed-up enforcement, and the lucrative rewards scammers can reap—a scam we investigated recently with ABC News *20/20* generated a reported $2 million *per week*—it's probably safe to predict that it will get worse before it gets better.

But that's the bad news. The good news is that there are many legitimate work-at-home jobs available, and we'll show you how to fine-tune your BS (Big Scam) Radar to protect yourself, and where to find the good leads, too.

Steer clear of ads waving red flags

Before you jump into the work-at-home trenches, you'll want to arm yourself with a few basic tools and plenty of common sense. To begin, here are some of the key red flags to watch out for as you assess an ad for a home-based job:

1. **"Work at Home" appears in the ad header.** Authentic job leads usually include a job title (Accountant, Security Guard, Bookkeeper, and so forth) at the beginning of the ad. "Work at home" and "work from home" are not job titles. If these phrases appear in the header (where the job title would normally appear), or otherwise dominate the ad, there's a good chance you're viewing a scam.

    These eye-grabbing phrases are the bait of the scammers' "hook" as they fish for desperate job seekers to reel in.

2. **Claims that no experience is necessary, and no resume is requested.** In the "real" world, employers usually require at least some degree of experience, and even for entry-level positions they'll often note criteria or preferences. Similarly, they'll typically ask for a resume or similar document.

    In the scam world, however, the target's desperation and need to believe are far more important than experience or skills. And listing any skill requirements puts the scammer at risk of thinning his victim pool.

3. **You're required to pay a fee.** Work is something you get paid to do, not something you pay for the privilege of doing. Even so, scammers have come up with countless ways to try to validate the fees they attach to their cons. For example, the charge is:

    ◆ "A processing fee."

    ◆ "A one-time intake fee."

    ◆ "To show us you're serious about the opportunity."

◆   "To cover the costs associated with sending you information about the position."

That said, there are a few exceptions to the don't pay for
home-based work rule. Because this book is about finding the
good jobs, we don't want you to "throw the baby out with the
bath water," so we'll pause a moment here to cover them.

For most people, the significant exceptions to the
"don't pay" rule occur in the virtual call center arena. Here,
some companies—legitimate firms such as LiveOps, Arise,
VIPdesk, and others—hire agents as independent contractors rather than employees. Due to IRS rules that define the
difference between the two statuses of worker and how a
company must interact with each, these employers may
sometimes require agents to pay for training or equipment, or
set up a limited liability company or corporation (at their own
expense) before starting work. Similarly, agents may have to
pay for a background and/or credit check.

For more detail on the differences between independent
contractors and employees, Google "independent contractors vs. employees," and see the IRS's Website at IRS.gov.

4. **Claims of enormous paychecks.** Here, anyone can be
tempted, but let common sense prevail. If brick-and-mortar
data-entry jobs, for example, pay minimum wage—as they
often do—how can an ad credibly claim that someone would
make $4,500 *a week* doing the same work from home—
part-time? Exaggerated claims of income are a sure sign of
a scam, especially when coupled with a "fee" to get started.
(Talk about gilding a lily!)

5. **The job ad or offer arrives as spam in your e-mail.**
Scamming and spamming go hand-in-hand. Your average
share-the-love con artist wants to distribute his wonderful
offer to as many people as possible (and of course, he has
to play the averages, too). Spam gives him a cheap path to
in-boxes around the world.

In the infamous "Angel Stevens" rebate processing
scam we investigated with *20/20*, we learned just how aggressive some scammer "spam campaigns" (we call them
Spampaigns) can be. One scammer sent out 68,000 spam
messages in *a single day.*

The moral? Though miracles do happen, they don't arrive via spam. If you receive unsolicited job offers in your e-mail, it's probably because a scammer purchased your e-mail address, or harvested it from another site.

A "trash" tip: When you dispose of the spam, be sure to move it to your trash file *without* using the "remove me from this list" link that you're likely to find at the bottom of the page. These links are often used to confirm that e-mail addresses are active, and clicking on them can result in even more spam.

6. **No job description.** Many work-at-home scam ads tell you repeatedly how much money you can make, how easy the work will be, and all the great things you can buy with those fanned-out $100 bills. What they don't tell you is what you'll be *doing*. (Or if they do, the reference is usually vague.) Real job listings will almost always tell you, if only briefly, what your duties will be.

7. **Palm trees, mansions, beaches, and bikinis.** It pains us to say it, but if the ad features palm trees, a mansion, beaches, and a Ferrari, it's probably a scam. Women in bikinis draped over a rotund, grinning guy? Definitely a scam. Stacks of money, too? Run for the hills.

   Successful scammers often bag their prey by dangling enticing things in front of them—much like kidnappers do: "Hey kid, if you get into my car I'll give you this candy bar."

8. **"Limited number of openings" in the subject line.** "We are seeking 11 people to work from home!" Scammers use this tactic to make the offer more vivid, and build a sense of urgency in their prospective marks: "If I don't act now, the opportunity may disappear!"

   As con men grow more tech-savvy, we've also seen an increase in Websites that feature a countdown clock. The clock ticks away the last minutes you have left before the "incredible opportunity" vanishes. (Don't worry; it won't. Refresh the page and the clock resets.)

9. **The ad makes you feel vaguely uneasy.** If an offer makes you feel a bit worried or anxious, and you find yourself trying to talk yourself into taking the plunge—stop, and go with your gut. Most of us have a pretty sharp survival instinct, that

stirs when something's not right. Resist the urge to override it—especially when reading work-at-home ads.

10. **They ask for everything but your first-born.** If the initial "application process" asks for one or more of the following, it's likely a scam: your Social Security number, bank account number, credit card number, passport number, or other similar information.

Although legitimate employers will need your Social Security number for tax purposes, they'll rarely if ever ask for it at a preliminary stage of recruitment.

Popular work-at-home scams

Scammers often run variations of scams, or park good ones on the shelf, then bring them back out for fresh prey. Familiarizing yourself with some of the more popular current work-at-home scams will help protect you now and in the future.

Rebate processing

This scam, which emerged in 2008, is still going strong. It's a classic bait and switch. The scammers imply that you'll be doing basic data-entry work, and making good money at it. But once they get your money, they eventually reveal that the "job" is actually commission-only affiliate sales. No sales, no income!

Auction listing processors

Following in the footsteps of its rebate-processing cousin (and often perpetrated by the same con men), this little dandy is spreading like wildfire.

Like the rebate processing scam, this one's a bait and switch, too. Again, you're lured in by the prospect of data entry–type work. But once you pay up, you discover you'll actually be a salesperson, and you won't make a penny unless you move products.

The "instant" online business (Biz-in-a-Box)

The Internet is littered with "Biz-in-a-Box" sites, like fast-food trash on the side of the road. They sport names like "wealth builder," "cash secret," and so on.

As the names suggest, the typical bait is impressive income for basic work—typing, data entry, placing ads with Google, and similar tasks. But the truth is you'll be selling everything from diets and vitamins to dating services, Website hosting services, and even other work-at-home scams!

Worse still, the "kit" or "system" is often hawked as "free," but the victim's credit card is immediately hit with ongoing monthly "consulting" or "Web hosting" fees of $39.99, $59.90, and so forth.

Check cashing/forwarding

In this devastating scam, the job seeker is told that his or her role is to receive checks, deposit them into a personal bank account, and wire the money to the hiring company, keeping a generous percentage for the sender's efforts. In reality, the checks, which often look perfectly legitimate, having been stolen from a bank, are bogus and will bounce, but not until after the victim has wired funds from his or her personal account to the scammer.

In the end, it's the victim who pays the price, as the funds have usually been wired abroad and can't be recovered, and the bank claims the victim's deposits.

Data entry

Unfortunately, this is a perennial bestseller. Scammers know that basic home-based administrative work is in high demand, and very scarce. (A few companies offer legitimate data-entry work, but their waiting lists can be literally years long.)

If you get an e-mail telling you how desperate a company is for qualified data-entry specialists, it's a scam. Don't try to talk yourself into believing it—just hit "delete."

"Get rich taking surveys"

Yes, you can make a little money—sporadically—taking surveys (usually $1 to $5, a bit more if it's a focus group). But contrary to the scammer's come-on, you should never pay a fee to take a survey, and you will not make a living at it.

Package forwarding

Postal forwarding losses are on the way to the $1 billion mark—and keep getting worse. In this scam, you agree to receive and repack electronics (MP3 players, video recorders, DVD players, and so on), fill out customs forms, and send the goods overseas. In exchange, the "hiring company" says it will pay you a fee, and reimburse you for shipping expenses.

The truth? You're a "fence," providing a cover of legitimacy for thieves buying goods with stolen credit cards. Not only will you not get paid, but you may well be arrested for shipping stolen goods, and for having entered fraudulent information on the customs forms. Stay away!

Mystery shopping*

Another perennial, but now with a nasty twist.

Back in the day, this scam usually involved selling victims an outdated list of companies who hired mystery shoppers. Now, scammers lure victims with a nice "cashier's check" to be used for shopping, often at an attractive upscale store such as Nordstrom. You deposit the apparently legitimate check, go shopping up to an inviting limit, then wire the remaining funds back to the scammers via MoneyGram or Western Union.

Later, the bank discovers the check is bogus, and now the only "mystery" is where the funds went, and how you're going to repay the bank for the shopping spree and the wire transfer. And just for dessert, you may have to answer federal questions about bank fraud.

*Legitimate mystery shopping jobs do exist. See Chapter 12 for details.

Order processor jobs (AKA "e-mail processing")

In this e-version of the classic envelope-stuffing scam, you're asked to pay a fee to learn how to make money processing orders from "ads that you place on the Internet." But your chance to "process orders" comes only when you turn into a scammer yourself, and send the same scam on to your own prospective victims. Not exactly the job most people are looking for (and it's a great way to lose friends).

Envelope stuffing

This oldie but baddie is still with us. Typically, the scammer charges you a fee to show you how to make money stuffing envelopes. Then, you either receive nothing at all, or a letter instructing you to place the same ad that you yourself replied to, so you can scam others the same way you were scammed.

There are many other scams, of course, but these examples will give you a sense of how most of them are run. The spots may change, but the leopard remains the same.

Steps you can take to find out if a company is legitimate

If you've looked for red flags and suspicious patterns, and still can't decide if a job lead is a scam—or you simply want to be sure you've checked a lead thoroughly—here are some steps to help seal the deal.

Conduct a simple search

One of the first research steps we always suggest to job seekers is to go to your favorite search engine, and type in the name of the job title or company, followed by "+" and "scam." (For example, try "rebate processing" + scam.) This will quickly turn up any scam complaints (both verified and unverified, so take what you find with a grain of salt) about the company or the lead.

Learn from others who have been scammed

When you're investigating a work-at-home opportunity, always stop by the free message boards at sites such as WorkPlaceLikeHome.com and WAHM.com, and check for relevant discussions. If someone has been scammed by the company or individual you're researching, chances are you will find the details, and can avoid the same mistake.

Be sure the puzzle pieces line up

Be leery of any ad that looks legitimate at first glance, with the name and Website address of a respected company, but includes only a "free" e-mail address (Hotmail, Gmail, and so on) for replies. Established companies such as Ashley Furniture and Michigan Supply Co. have been victimized by scammers who use their names and reputations to sucker in unwitting job seekers.

In the same vein, always stop by the company Website for a look around before responding to a job ad. (You should develop this habit anyway, to learn more about the employer's corporate culture, so you can tailor your cover letter and resume accordingly.) In the Ashley Furniture and Michigan Supply cases, notices were posted warning visitors of the scam.

Check with the Better Business Bureau

There are essentially two ways to get listed with the BBB: buy a membership, or get reported for poor business practices.

Although the absence of a company's name in their listings is not unusual or suspect (not every business is a paying member of the BBB), a firm with a C, D, or F rating and multiple complaints deserves a flashing warning signal in your job search.

Research scam-specific sites

You can also visit such sites as ComplaintsBoard.com, Scam.com, IveTriedThat.com, and RipOffReport.com to check for relevant complaints. These sites often include a wealth of detail on emerging scams and scammers, and can help you avoid a nasty experience.

What to do if you're scammed

In the unlikely event you fall victim to a work-at-home scam *after* you read this book (we say this only partly tongue-in-cheek, as scammers are becoming more sophisticated by the day), here are some steps you can take to mitigate the damage.

Although the odds of recovering funds may be small, *any* action is better than none, and only action can lead to stronger enforcement, better remedies, and a safer work-at-home marketplace for all.

◆ Keep all receipts of transactions, e-mails, notes of telephone conversations, and so forth. These will be key as you take further steps.

◆ If the scammer has your credit card number, call your bank or credit card company immediately, and have them cancel that account and issue you a new number and card.

◆ Check to see if the credit card company can do a "charge-back" for any funds you may have lost.

- ◆ If scammers have your bank account number, contact your bank at once to close the account and open one with a new number.

- ◆ Unless advised by authorities to do otherwise, cease all contact with the scammer immediately. (Con artists are gifted "persuaders," and losses can quickly mount.)

- ◆ Report the crime, notifying:
  - ◆ The FBI via the Internet Crime Complaint Center (IC3.gov).
  - ◆ The Federal Trade Commission (FTC.gov).
  - ◆ Your local law-enforcement authorities.
  - ◆ Your state's attorney general (AG) and, if you know the state where the scam originates, the AG there as well (naag.org).
  - ◆ Your state's agency for consumer protection.

- ◆ The Better Business Bureau.

- ◆ Write your local, state and federal political representatives, requesting stronger enforcement of consumer-protection laws.

- ◆ Continue to self-educate, so you won't be a victim again!

- ◆ Share your experience with others online.

Now that your BS Radar is tuned and ready to sound an alert at the first sign of a scam, let's start looking for job leads!

CHAPTER 5

Good and Bad Work-at-Home Job Search Terms

"I don't search; I find," Picasso famously said. Here, we'll show you how to conduct Picasso-grade searches, with phrases that focus results dramatically, and reduce the number of scams. By the end of this chapter, you'll be armed with dozens of strategic search terms to help secure you a winning position in the job race.

All search terms are not created equal

With the right search terms, Google and other search engines can work marvelously to turn up telework job leads. But like the human mind, search engines function largely as "garbage in, garbage out" machines. Fill them with the wrong information, and they'll spew out data that's of little use.

Unfortunately, the majority of job seekers put themselves at significant competitive disadvantage by searching with such phrases as "work from home" and "work at home." Indeed, these phrases are almost toxic, yielding millions of undifferentiated hits, many of them scams.

And yet, simply tweaking the phrase to "this is a work-from-home position" narrows the field and ups the quality considerably. But why?

Though "work at home" and "work from home" are common hooks for scammers, the revised phrase mirrors language often used by human resources personnel and other staff when they write job ads. Because scams overwhelmingly outnumber legitimate job leads, thinking like an HR manager rather than a job seeker will help you separate good apples from a bushel of bad.

A glance at the basics

If you haven't searched often, we'll pause a moment for the basics. Here are two you'll want to keep in mind before you dig in:

1. When searching for an exact phrase, such as "must be willing to work from home," put the phrase in quotation marks. This instructs the search engine to look for the identical phrase across the Internet.

    If you enter the same phrase, "must be willing to work from home," without the quotes, the search will return Web pages containing the same phrase, but will also return pages containing the individual words in the phrase. For example, your results might include "We left our <u>home</u> in New York on Tuesday and, with some hard <u>work</u>, we reached Texas on Thursday. The stars <u>must</u> <u>be</u> aligned and, God <u>willing</u>, we will reach…."

2. Insert the plus sign (+) between your search terms to find job listings that contain multiple terms or phrases. For example, you might use "from home" + "customer service" to find home-based call center jobs. (You'll find more on this shortly.)

    There are many other tips and tricks for making the most of search engines, but these are the two we'll be relying on here. If you'd like to learn more, just search with terms such as "search engine basics" or "search engine commands."

Creating brilliant search phrases

Now let's put on for a moment that HR manager's hat we alluded to earlier. If an HR manager were writing an ad for your ideal position, what would he or she be likely to say? Better still, if you've come across ads for a perfect position, how were they worded? Did they contain phrases you could recycle in an effective search? (Phrases are a bit like combinations to safes: They unlock the door to the gems. Individual words alone, on the other hand, are often too common to be effective search terms.)

In our many years of researching home-based jobs, the following search terms and phrases have proved among the most effective for finding legitimate job leads. (Bear in mind, however, that even the best search terms don't eliminate scams altogether, so be sure to keep your "BS" radar on.)

As you try these searches yourself, experiment with swapping out certain words for similar terms. For example, in many cases similar words such as *telecommute, telecommuting, telework,* and *teleworking* can be interchanged to sharpen your search and produce additional useful hits. (For an "interchange" illustration, see the first two bulleted examples in the following list.)

Likewise, where we've used the phrase "work from home," be sure to try "work at home," too, for different results. Just changing the preposition can open a different safe. (Other possible word exchanges—where they make sense, of course—include must/should, may/can, is/will be, and position/job/opening.)

- ◆ "this is a telecommuting position"
    - ◆ "this is a teleworking position"
    - ◆ "this is a telecommute position"
    - ◆ "this is a telework position"
- ◆ "telecommuting may be possible"
    - ◆ "teleworking may be possible"
    - ◆ "telecommute may be possible"
    - ◆ "telework may be possible"
- ◆ "full telecommute"
- ◆ "partial telecommute"
- ◆ "full telecommuting position"
- ◆ "telecommuting available"
- ◆ "telecommute from anywhere"
- ◆ "option to telecommute"
- ◆ "this is a home-based position"
- ◆ "this home-based position" *(With the words* is a *removed, this phrase will return leads with text such as "<u>this home-based position</u> requires high-speed Internet.")*
- ◆ "must have home office"
- ◆ "must have a home office set-up"
- ◆ "must use your own office equipment"
- ◆ "must have quiet home office"

- "qualified individual will work from home"
- "home office with up-to-date computer"
- "candidate will work from home"
- "candidate will work from a home office"
- "must be willing to work from home"
- "option to work from home"
- "this is a work from home position"
- "our employees work from home"
- "our staff works from home"
- "remote work from home"
- "hiring home-based"
- "is seeking a home-based"
- "must have a quiet work space"
- "must have high-speed Internet"
- "must have your own PC"
- "this is a remote position"
- "1099 position"
- "this is a 1099 position"
- "independent contractor position"
- "virtual office arrangement"
- "remote contractor"
- "we are seeking a freelance" *(This open-ended phrase will turn up all sorts of freelance positions, but you can fine-tune by adding the type of freelance position you're searching for. For example "we are seeking a freelance blogger" or "we are seeking a freelance translator.")*
- "off-site position"
- "this is an off-site position"
- "virtual company"
- "we are a virtual business"
- "we are a virtual company"
- "this is a virtual position"
- "work may be done virtually"
- "you may work virtually"
- "this is a freelance position"

◆ "will be a contract worker"

◆ "will be an independent contractor"

◆ "this is an independent contractor position"

◆ "may work from anywhere" *(You can add geographical param-eters if you wish: "may work from anywhere in the world," " in the U.S.," " in California," and so on.)*

◆ "can work from anywhere" *(As above, and you can also change "may" to "can" to accommodate different writing styles.)*

◆ "position can be based anywhere" *(See above.)*

◆ "this is an off-site position"

◆ "will work from your own office"

◆ "this is an Internet-based job"

◆ "work from your own location"

A plus sign can yield specific jobs

If you're looking for a specific type of position, you can create com-bination searches to ferret out the leads. To illustrate, let's say you're inter-ested in a home-based customer service job. We can assume that a typical ad for that position might include several points:

◆ Applicants will need a quiet workspace.

◆ The work will be done from home.

◆ Applicants will need high-speed Internet access.

Now, it's just a matter of choosing the phrases you feel will work best, putting them in quotation marks, and stringing them together with one or more plus (+) signs. (Using the + symbol instructs the search engine to look for individual pages that contain all of the exact phrases. Though the hits may not always be precisely what you're looking for, it's a great way to narrow down your search.) In this case, we'd try:

"customer service" + "from home" + "quiet work space"

If the first + combination doesn't yield what you need, try removing one part of the formula, or changing it up a bit:

"customer service" + "from home"

"customer service" + "at home"

"customer service" + telecommute

"customer service" + "high-speed Internet"

"customer service" + "home-based"

"customer service" + "quiet home office"

Don't be afraid to experiment. When you find the type of ads you're looking for, be sure to read them thoroughly, and jot down any key phrases you should add to your search list.

Getting an edge with advanced search options

Most popular search engines have advanced search options that few people know about, and even fewer use. If you're serious about using search engines in your job hunt, you'll want to tap into these advanced features.

In most cases, you'll find the link to advanced search options on the same page you use for standard searches. Look for a link labeled "advanced," "advanced search," or something similar.

The following are the four most popular search engines, with instructions to access their advanced search options.

◆ **Google.com** Click on the "advanced search" link to the right of the search field.

◆ **Yahoo.com** At the home page, leave the search field blank, and click on the "web search" button. On the next page, click on the "options" link, and on the succeeding page, in the drop-down menu, select "advanced search."

◆ **Bing.com** As we write, this next-generation replacement for the Microsoft MSN/Live search application is in its fledgling stages, making changes likely. For the moment, the "advanced" search options can be reached only after you've done a basic search. Then, at the top of the page, just below and to the right of the "search" field, you'll find the "advanced" link.

◆ **Ask.com** Click on the "advanced" link below the search field.

Making the most of Google

If Sonny the mascot was "cuckoo for Cocoa Puffs," then we're "ga-ga for Google." It's the search engine we use most, because it's both simple and comprehensive, with features that do a lot of the work for us.

One of our favorite advanced search features is Google's "date" option, which lets you do a "freshness" search, and request only those pages that have been added or updated in the past 24 hours, the past week, the past month, and so forth. It's a great way to weed out stale job listings, or leads you've already seen, and focus on new leads, which are more likely to be open. (As we've mentioned, legitimate work-at-home jobs fill very quickly.)

Here's how to use the "date" feature:

◆   Go to Google.com.

◆   Click on the "advanced search" link.

◆   In the field labeled "this exact wording or phrase," type in (just as an example) "this is a telecommuting position," but without the quotes, as using this field automatically instructs the search engine to look for this exact phrase.

◆   Scrolling down the page, click on the link that reads "Date, usage rights, numeric range, and more," and new options will appear.

◆   From the drop-down menu in the "date" field, select "past 24 hours."

◆   Scroll down and click the "advanced search" button.

Bonus tip: You can even rank these results, too, by "freshness," putting the newest leads at the top of the list. Simply click on the "show options" link above your search results, then select "sort by date" from the left column.

In our example, you'll now see only those Web pages that (1) feature the phrase "this is a telecommuting position," and (2) have been created or updated in the past 24 hours.

To appreciate the advantages of the "freshness" feature, try the search again without the date parameters. You'll see how it can save you from getting bogged down in hundreds of stale job leads and references.

Let Google Alerts
"search while you sleep"

Another of our favorite Google tools is Google Alerts (*www.google.com/alerts*), which notifies users by e-mail when their specified search terms appear on the Internet. The "hits" are gathered by Google software units known as "bots," which scour Web pages continuously, looking for new references to the words or phrases you've entered.

To illustrate, let's say you set a Google Alert for the search term "work at home," and you request to be notified "as-it-happens" (other options include "once a day" or "once a week"). Every time the phrase pops up on Websites, online news channels, blogs, job boards, and so on, Google will send you an e-mail alert with a link to the page, along with a few lines of the text in which the phrase appears.

In setting Google Alerts, or searching Google generally, you can even keep track of new entries appearing on a specific Website by using the "site:" command. For example, if you want to be notified of new telecommuting job leads posted to the Idealist.org Website (a source of nonprofit jobs; see Chapter 6), you would set your alert for:

"telecommuting position" site:idealist.org

In your research, as you decide which search words and phrases work best for you, we encourage you to set up Google Alerts for each. Not only will you feel better at having a platoon of little helpers out mining the Net for job leads, they work for free, they don't complain, they don't leave their dirty clothes lying around, and they don't play video games when they should be doing their homework.

CHAPTER 6

Jobs by Type and Where to Find Them

In this chapter, we'll share some of the best places to find home-based work. We've categorized each site by job type, so you can quickly identify and explore the areas that interest you most. But we encourage you to explore other job categories, too. Sometimes, the perfect job is one we haven't considered!

Making the most of these resources

As you know, information on the Internet changes quickly, which makes book authors everywhere rightfully leery of including online resources that could morph overnight. Accordingly, our goal in the Website lists that follow and in this book generally has been to include only those companies that have (1) been in business for a while, (2) maintained a reliable Web presence, and (3) acquired a reputation as legitimate hirers of home-based workers. Though no one of course can *guarantee* such things (even the immortal General Motors declared bankruptcy, and managements are always subject to change), we've done our best to ensure that the resources you find here will be both reliable and accessible.

In the same vein, the URLs or Web links included in this chapter are for Website home pages rather than for specific "employment" or "careers" pages, whose links are more likely to change.

But navigating from a site's home page to its job leads is usually fairly simple. Begin by looking for a tab or link labeled "jobs," "careers," or "employment," and click on it. Absent those options, try clicking the "about us" or "company" link, then look for a link to jobs on the succeeding page. (If a company has placed its jobs in a less-obvious location, we've included tips on where to find them, according to their Website layouts as we go to press. We have avoided giving minute details, however, not from haste or carelessness, but again because Websites can so often change.)

For each job category, we've also included a brief "backgrounder," and some points for you to consider as you delve in. Additionally, we've listed some searches you may want to try, so you can explore beyond the sites we've noted, and maximize your options. (As we've said, well-crafted searches can take you to solid job leads that might not be found in the usual places.) Although numerous, our suggested search phrases are meant to be thought starters rather than definitive catalogues, so be sure to experiment with some of your own, and keep track of those that yield the best results.

We've also gathered "insider tips" from companies and experts in selected job areas. Be sure to take their advice and wisdom into account as you weigh your choices and chart your path.

For each site we've listed, you'll also find the following:

◆ Company name.

◆ Link to the company's Website.

◆ "Site type": the nature of the site, such as staffing agency, direct hire (that is, the employer's own site), industry-specific job board, and so forth.

◆ "How to use": our notes on how to find jobs on the site. The instruction "View posted positions" indicates a conventional or obvious path to advertised positions.

◆ "Positions/work": the types of positions or work the company may have available, based on historical data. *Note that recruiting needs are often volatile, and companies may or may not be hiring at this time.*

◆ "In their words": a brief descriptive quote taken from the Website. (Some have been edited lightly for punctuation.)

For certain sites you'll also find an "Authors' note," where we share any relevant inside information or opinions we may have about the company.

And speaking of notes, please note that here and elsewhere in the book we've intentionally omitted or minimized references to hourly wages, salaries, and other compensation information. Similar to links to specific Web pages, these too are subject to frequent change. For current pay rates, see the FAQ sections of employer Websites, and discussions of specific positions on sites such as WorkPlaceLikeHome.com and WAHM.com. For customer-service position pay rates, see our chart at *www.ratracerebellion.com/ CS_Comparison.html*.

We and HR managers around the world are begging you...

We'd be remiss if we didn't mention a frequent and flagrant (but easily avoided) misstep in the job-hunting world. Human resources (HR) managers increasingly complain that job seekers have not taken the time to read the job description thoroughly, or review the company Website before applying for a position. Too often, applicants disregard geographical restrictions related to the job, technical specifications, scheduling conditions, experience requirements, and even clear statements on the site that a position has been filled, or that "applications are not being accepted at this time."

This not only burdens the HR manager with unnecessary work, but it also singles out the applicant as someone who is slipshod or negligent, and who can't follow directions. Worse yet, it gives telework and teleworkers generally a bad name. Therefore, on behalf of HR managers around the world—and knowing as we do the importance of telework to so many deserving individuals and families, if not to the environment of the entire globe—we beseech you to do your homework before applying for a job. Take the time to explore the company Website and learn whatever you can about the company's culture, its services or products, the conditions attached to any position, and, last but not least, whether an opening actually exists, and the company wants to see your application.

The moral of our sermon? *He who looks first, looks best.*

Work-at-home sites by job type

Before we get to the nitty-gritty, please note that the listing of a resource here shouldn't imply that we endorse its mission, values, and so forth, nor does the exclusion of any hirer imply a lack of trust. Also, in addition to the sites here, you may want to check our ever-changing list of screened hirers and jobs at RatRaceRebellion.com, our usual "online home."

Accounting and financial

Most accounting and financial jobs are "data-driven"—making them ideal for home-based work.

Positions in this industry usually require special training and/or licensing. However, we occasionally see leads for support positions as well.

Considerations:

◆   Will require a quiet environment for focus on the work.

◆   Companies may require that you possess or install encryption or security applications to protect sensitive data.

Searches you may want to try:

◆   accountant + "from home"

◆   accountant + "from home" + job

◆   bookkeeper + "from home" + job

◆   CPA + "at home"

◆   accountant + telecommute

Insider Tip

Thomas Joseph, Founder, Bookminders:

"People interested in getting into the home-based bookkeeping field, or any home-based business for that matter, need to remember that there can be a significant administrative burden required to market, manage, and bill for your services. Employees of Bookminders enjoy a work-life balance because our organization provides the infrastructure so that employees can focus on practicing their craft. The challenge in employing home-workers is to do it in a way that is easy to manage."

Accountants, Inc.	accountantsinc.com	
	Site type:	Staffing and recruiting.
	How to use:	Use the search feature. Try keywords: telecommute, home, freelance, offsite, virtual, remote.
	Positions/ work:	Accountants and various financial staff positions.
	In their words:	"Accountants, Inc. offers a full range of accounting and finance employment opportunities on a project, project to direct hire, and direct hire basis."

Balance Your Books	balanceyourbooks.com	
	Site type:	Direct hire.
	How to use:	View posted positions.
	Positions/work:	Accounting, bookkeeping, sales, appointment setting.
	In their words:	"Balance Your Books provides outsourced online bookkeeping and controllership services to small, mid-size, and fast-growing businesses."

Bookminders	bookminders.com	
	Site type:	Direct hire.
	How to use:	View posted positions.
	Positions/work:	Accounting, sales.
	In their words:	"Bookminders is the premier provider of outsourced accounting and information management services for small businesses and nonprofit organizations, and is dedicated to being an industry leader in utilizing a home-based workforce."

CHMB	chmbsolutions.com	
	Site type:	Direct hire.
	How to use:	View posted positions.
	Positions/ work:	Account specialists for the medical field.
	In their words:	"Today, CHMB provides a comprehensive slate of business services to more than 1,000 physicians in 200 medical practices throughout Southern California, representing numerous surgical, primary care and internal medicine specialties."

ClickNwork	clicknwork.com	
Authors' note: This company offers a variety of positions, so be sure to roam around while you're at their site.	Site type:	Direct hire.
	How to use:	View posted positions.
	Positions/work:	Analysts, consultants.
	In their words:	"We are always on the lookout for good analysts (consultants, economists, etc.) that can assist in a range of assignments. These include undertaking various forms of market and financial analysis and preparing company profiles, market reviews and economic papers."

First Data	firstdata.com	
	Site type:	Direct hire.
	How to use:	Search for positions. Try keywords: home, remote.
	Positions/work:	Account executive.
	In their words:	"First Data Corp. is a leading provider of electronic commerce and payment solutions for businesses worldwide, with operation in 37 countries. First Data serves over 5.4 million merchant locations, over 2,000 card issuers and their customers."
OSI Business Services	osibusinessservices.com	
	Site type:	Direct hire.
	How to use:	View posted positions. The jobs link is on their "resources" menu.
	Positions/work:	Accountant, bookkeeper, sales.
	In their words:	"Our mission is to enable our clients to focus on those activities by providing them with a full-service outsourced accounting department to handle everything from daily bookkeeping tasks to weekly, monthly and annual financial reporting."

VT Audit	vtaudit.com	
	Site type:	Direct hire.
	How to use:	View posted positions.
	Positions/work:	Auditors.
	In their words:	"If you have experience in processing payroll, or you have worked with bills of lading in shipping and receiving, you can join our team of home-based auditors creating workers compensation and/or general liability audits for Property & Casualty Insurance clients nationwide."

Administrative, clerical, and data entry

For decades or more, people have "taken in typing" and other clerical tasks, working at spare tables in the home and offering up the finished product by hand. As in so many areas of work, the Internet has wrought a revolution here, creating everything from virtual assistants to remote desktop publishing, and eliminating the automobile that shuttled the paperwork to and fro.

Considerations:

◆ Administrative, clerical, and data-entry positions are among the most sought-after home-based jobs. Prepare for stiff competition. Waiting lists can be long.

◆ If you prefer to work for yourself, consider becoming a virtual assistant. For reference, see our manual, *The 2-Second Commute: Join the Exploding Ranks of Freelance Virtual Assistants* (Career Press, 2005), available on Amazon, at Barnes & Noble, and in some public libraries.

◆ Data entry is one of the most scam-ridden sectors of the work-at-home arena, so exercise caution, and *never* pay a fee to work.

Searches you may want to try:

◆ "administrative assistant" + "from home"

◆ "word processing" + "from home"

Insider Tip

Diane Dion, President, DionData Solutions:

"Take your home-based data entry career seriously. Have patience, perseverance, and a professional attitude. This is your business and your integrity is on the line."

Axion Data Services	axiondata.com	
Authors' note: Data-entry hirers are often swamped with applications, so be sure to check the site to see if Axion is hiring. If they are not, do not call or e-mail, but (as with other sites) check back and apply when appropriate.	Site type:	Direct hire.
	How to use:	View posted positions.
	Positions/work:	Data entry.
	In their words:	"All data-entry operators work from home and are independent contractors. Contractors provide their own computer equipment and software, pay their own taxes, and bill Axion for the work performed."
Capital Typing	capitaltyping.com	
	Site type:	Direct hire.
	How to use:	View posted positions.
	Positions/work:	Administrative support, data entry, translation, transcription, customer service.
	In their words:	"Capital Typing is an outsourcing company providing premium value outsourcing services and virtual office support."

DionData Solutions	diondatasolutions.net/opportunities.htm	
	Site type:	Direct hire.
	How to use:	View posted positions.
	Positions/work:	Data entry.
	In their words:	"DionData Solutions is a legitimate Data Management Service Bureau. We provide all training and programs at NO cost to you, with no requested hidden fees of any kind."
Expedict *Authors' note: This company is based in the UK, but hires from around the world.*	expedict.co.uk	
	Site type:	Direct hire
	How to use:	View posted positions.
	Positions/work:	Audio typists
	In their words:	"Expedict is the home for experienced audio typists who want to be part of a young, fast-growing, professional organisation. We operate mainly (but not exclusively) in the financial, communications, and legal fields."
KeyForCash *Authors' note: We've heard that KeyForCash can have long waiting lists, so you may have to wait a while, or even reapply.*	keyforcash.com	
	Site type:	Direct hire.
	How to use:	View posted positions.
	Positions/work:	Data entry.
	In their words:	"KeyForCash is a website that enables you to earn money by typing at home. We are in the business of data entry services, which means we have a lot of data that we need to be entered into computers. We show you the data, you type it in."

Mulberry Studio	mulberrystudio.com	
	Site type:	Direct hire.
	How to use:	View posted positions.
	Positions/work:	Transcription, proofreading.
	In their words:	"People at Mulberry Studio tend to stay. During life changes, Mulberry Studio will work with you to provide the flexibility you need. We are loyal to our staff and our staff is loyal to us."
OfficeTeam	officeteam.com	
	Site type:	Staffing service.
	How to use:	Use the job search feature to look for home-based positions. Try keywords: home, virtual, telecommute, telecommuting, remote.
	Positions/work:	Administrative, various.
	In their words:	"OfficeTeam is the world's largest specialized temporary staffing service for administrative professionals."
Team Double-Click®	teamdoubleclick.com	
	Site type:	Direct hire.
	How to use:	View posted positions.
	Positions/work:	Virtual assistants.
	In their words:	"We are a virtual staffing agency, working with thousands of the best professional virtual office assistants the world has to offer."

Adult texter/phone actress

Given its controversial nature, we hemmed and hawed about whether to include this section. However, in view of the number of queries we've received throughout the years about adult texting and phone acting jobs, and our aim to offer a comprehensive guide, we decided in the affirmative.

We understand, of course, that this type of work isn't for everyone, so please feel free to scroll down to the next category. Otherwise, for those who are interested, it's reported that some people are making excellent money in this field, though hours may be long.

Considerations:

◆ It almost goes without saying, phone actress jobs are best done when there are no children in the house!

◆ Must be at least 18 years old.

◆ Usually requires a corded telephone (no cordless or cell phones).

◆ Commonly referred to as "PSOs" (phone sex operators).

Searches you may want to try:

◆ "phone actress" + "at home"

◆ "adult chat" + "from home"

◆ "adult texting" + "from home" + job

◆ "phone sex" + "from home" + job

Insider Tip

"Happyfingers," Forum Administrator, Textilicious.com:

"The main thing people getting into PSO work need to know is that to make this work and make ends meet, they will probably be working far longer hours then they ever did working outside of the home. I log in on average 16 + hours a day for PSO work. (Luckily with PSO work those hours fly by, not so much with texting though!)"

1800Delilah	1800delilah.com	
	Site type:	Direct hire.
	How to use:	View posted positions.
	Positions/work:	Phone actress.
	In their words:	"1800Delilah pays a minimum of \$.50/min. or \$30.00 per talk hour. If you select phones and Internet, you will receive additional calls, as many of our callers check our website before calling."
The Boulevard Entertainment, Inc.	blvdent.com	
	Site type:	Direct hire.
	How to use:	View posted positions.
	Positions/work:	Phone actress.
	In their words:	"The Boulevard Entertainment, Inc. is one of the most recognized and prestigious adult telephone entertainment companies, specializing in one-on-one erotic adult conversations for the last 19 years."
Madamay	madamay.com	
	Site type:	Direct hire.
	How to use:	View posted positions.
	Positions/work:	Phone actors and actresses.
	In their words:	"Easily make yourself available or unavailable for calls anytime you like. No need to check in with us or keep to a preset schedule. Our automated call system ensures that you will only receive calls from Madamay when you make yourself available for calls."

Papillon Agency	papillonagency.com	
	Site type:	Direct hire.
	How to use:	View posted positions.
	Positions/work:	Text chat operators, phone actresses.
	In their words:	"Our philosophy is that 'any job that you love is a job to be proud of.' Unlike many companies, we establish a sense of belonging! We run our company like a family, and frankly many of us have been here so long, we kind of are a 'FAMILY.'"
Phone Actress	phoneactress.com	
	Site type:	Direct hire.
	How to use:	View posted positions.
	Positions/work:	Phone actress.
	In their words:	"We are the nation's largest no-fee recruitment site for Internet and Telephone Actresses & Actors! Start your exciting career in adult entertainment while maintaining complete anonymity."
Phone Entertainers	phoneentertainers.com	
	Site type:	Direct hire.
	How to use:	View posted positions.
	Positions/work:	Phone actress.
	In their words:	"Our company prides itself on providing, and maintaining, a superior service for our clients. Our entertainers are not only well compensated, but are treated with kindness and respect."

Sexy Jobline	sexyjobline.com	
	Site type:	Direct hire.
	How to use:	View posted positions.
	Positions/work:	Phone actress.
	In their words:	"You will be engaging in conversation of a sexually explicit nature with our clients. We are a dispatch service; all calls will be routed directly to you from the company so you will remain completely anonymous."
Text121Chat	text121chat.com	
	Site type:	Direct hire.
	How to use:	View posted positions.
	Positions/work:	Text chat operators, phone actresses.
	In their words:	"As a leading independent adult texting company, Text121Chat has the expertise and experience you need. When it comes to the very best in interactive media solutions and premium rate operator services, we provide a wide range of specialized call centre services."

Textilicious	textilicious.com	
	Site type:	Niche-specific message board/ forum.
	How to use:	View and post messages regarding jobs and hiring companies.
	Positions/work:	Text chat operators, phone actresses.
	In their words:	"We are a forum for alternative and traditional work at home ladies (and a few gentlemen!). We would love to have you as part of our community."

Appointment setting and sales

These positions typically involve outbound phone calling, so make sure you really enjoy spending time on the telephone, and can handle rejection. A great phone voice and personality—along with excellent sales skills—will help you find success in this arena.

Considerations:

◆ As with many home-based jobs, this type of work
will require a quiet environment free of distractions.
Nobody (but especially someone you are "cold calling")
wants to hear screaming children, yowling dogs, or low-
flying planes in the background, so be sure to assess
your environment frankly before applying.

◆ Pay arrangements range from hourly to base plus salary
to commission only, depending on employer.

Searches you may want to try:

◆ "appointment setting" + "from home"

◆ "lead generation" + "from home"

◆ telemarketing + "from home"

Insider Tip

Brian Parnell, President and Founder, Grindstone Inc.:

"Business to Business Telemarketing and Telesales is not for everyone. You have to be outgoing and confident, and willing to make cold calls. If you have the skills, working from the comfort of your home office can be very rewarding. Grindstone Inc. is a highly professional company managing work at home agents."

AccuConference	accuconference.com	
	Site type:	Direct hire.
	How to use:	View posted positions.
	Positions/work:	Outside sales representatives.
	In their words:	"A pioneer in audio and web conferencing, AccuConference offers first-class customer service and support. The company prides itself in hiring outstanding individuals who are results-driven, and who take ownership of their work."
ARO *Authors' note: We've heard great things about ARO, and they offer a variety of work-at-home positions.*	callcenteroptions.com	
	Site type:	Direct hire.
	How to use:	View posted positions.
	Positions/work:	Customer service, premium auditors, sales, B2B marketing/telesales
	In their words:	"ARO is a contact center for some of the nation's leading corporations. We strive to provide an unmatched quality of customer care and business management to our clients with virtual technology."

Blue Zebra	bluezebraappointmentsetting.com	
Authors' note: Excellent reputation. Must have 2+ years of outbound, B2B cold-calling and appointment-setting experience.	Site type:	Direct hire.
	How to use:	View posted positions.
	Positions/work:	Business-to-business appointment setting.
	In their words:	"Professional cold calling and appointment setting, B2B, work from home, telecommute, independent contractor. This job opportunity entails cold calling or prospecting to set qualified appointments for our clients."

Cruise.com	cruise.com	
	Site type:	Direct hire.
	How to use:	View posted positions.
	Positions/work:	Sales, customer service.
	In their words:	"Cruise.com, Inc. was launched in 1998 and is the largest web site specializing in cruises on the Internet. We sell more cruises due to our advanced search and booking technology, greater content and discount prices (lower than all other major cruise sellers)."

Extended Presence	extendedpresence.com	
	Site type:	Direct hire.
	How to use:	View posted positions.
	Positions/work:	Appointment setting, lead generation.
	In their words:	"Extended Presence is a professional Sales Outsourcing and Lead Generation company that specializes in developing and managing outsourced sales and marketing programs for large technology companies."

Grindstone *Authors' note: This company has strict hiring criteria, so read carefully before applying.*	grindstone.com	
	Site type:	Direct hire.
	How to use:	View posted positions.
	Positions/work:	Telemarketers, appointment setters.
	In their words:	"Our clients demand that we hire the best. Those who pass our thorough screening process will have the opportunity to flourish with a growing company. We are on the cutting edge of a new trend, and we believe in promoting from within."

TeleReach	telereachjobs.com	
Authors' note: We've heard good things about this company. Be sure to check their FAQ to see if they are hiring in your geographical area.	Site type:	Direct hire.
	How to use:	View posted positions.
	Positions/work:	Appointment setting, lead generation.
	In their words:	"TeleReach Corporate, based in Houston, is a business development, appointment setting, lead generation and information gathering company. Since 1996 TeleReach has helped privately held and Fortune 100 client businesses...."

teleXpertise	telexpertise.com	
	Site type:	Direct hire.
	How to use:	View posted positions.
	Positions/work:	Sales/lead generation, team leaders, call evaluators, telephonic mystery shoppers.
	In their words:	"Over the years, we have become committed to the idea that the essence of evaluating a call is to evaluate it from the customer's perspective first."

Artistic

We've included links to sites with a variety of artistic or esthetically oriented jobs, including photography, illustration, greeting card design, doll artists, and others.

Considerations:

◆   Much of the work in this area is done on a freelance (independent contractor) basis.

Searches you may want to try:

◆   illustrator + "freelance position"

◆   "freelance artist" + job

◆ "seeking a freelance photographer"
◆ "looking for a freelance illustrator"

3D Tour	3dtour.com	
	Site type:	Direct hire.
	How to use:	View posted positions.
	Positions/work:	3D Tour photographers.
	In their words:	"We stand apart from other virtual tour companies due to the quality of our images, national coverage and personalized service."
Art Deadlines List	artdeadlineslist.com	
	Site type:	Job board.
	How to use:	View posted positions.
	Positions/work:	Various artistic jobs and opportunities.
	In their words:	"Art contests and competitions, art jobs and internships, art scholarships and grants and fellowships, art festivals, call for entries/proposals/projects, and other opportunities, in all disciplines, for art students, art teachers, and artists of all ages."
Avanti Press, Inc.	avantipress.com	
	Site type:	Direct hire.
	How to use:	Review submission guidelines found in the "contact" section.
	Positions/work:	Photography, writing.
	In their words:	"Avanti Press, Inc. has been publishing award-winning greetings sold around the world for over 25 years!"

The Bradford Group	thebradfordgroup.com	
Authors' note: Also hires doll artists for the Ashton-Drake Galleries.	Site type:	Direct hire.
	How to use:	View posted positions.
	Positions/work:	Freelance designers, illustrators, artists.
	In their words:	"The Bradford Group is seeking talented freelance designers, illustrators, and artists to work with our Product Development teams on innovative, unique collectible products, including collector plates from The Bradford Exchange, ornaments and music boxes from Bradford Editions, cottages from Hawthorne Village, and figurines from The Hamilton Collection."
DragonPencil	dragonpencil.com	
	Site type:	Direct hire.
	How to use:	View posted positions.
	Positions/work:	Illustrators.
	In their words:	"DragonPencil is always looking for the best illustrators in the world. We accept submissions from artists all over the globe."

Leanin' Tree	tradeleanintree.com	
	Site type:	Direct hire.
	How to use:	View posted positions.
	Positions/work:	Artists; verse writers.
	In their words:	"Leanin' Tree greeting cards have been an American tradition since 1949. That's when Ed Trumble, founder and Chairman, started selling Christmas cards through the mail to western farmers and ranchers...."

metaphor	metaphorstudio.com	
Authors' note: Yep, we know the "m" in their name is lowercase. That's how they use it!	Site type:	Direct hire.
	How to use:	View posted positions.
	Positions/work:	Freelance designers, illustrators, flash artists, flash animators, copywriters.
	In their words:	"metaphor is a full-service brand consultancy that provides identity, interactive, advertising and public relations."

Oatmeal Studios	oatmealstudios.com	
	Site type:	Direct hire.
	How to use:	View posted positions, review artists' guidelines.
	Positions/work:	Artists; writers.
	In their words:	"We are looking for fresh and fun-looking artwork in any media and style. Also, sophisticated, funky cartoony-type art (people and/or animals) with or without words."

Victory Productions	victoryprd.com	
	Site type:	Direct hire.
	How to use:	View posted positions.
	Positions/work:	Freelance writers, editors, proofreaders, designers, compositors, photographers, illustrators.
	In their words:	"Victory has grown each year thanks to the repeat business of our publishing clients, who have come to rely on Victory as an extension of their in-house teams and resources."

Call center and customer service

Virtual call centers (aka "homeshoring companies") present one of the fastest-growing opportunities for job seekers looking for home-based work. Here, we list some of our favorites, including those that have received rave reviews from people who have e-mailed us directly. We've also tried to focus on those companies that don't impose narrow geographical restrictions.

To find more companies like these at our RatRaceRebellion.com Website, click on the "call center and customer service" link.

Considerations:

◆ As with any job that involves extensive conversation with customers on the phone, these positions require a quiet work environment.

◆ Some call centers hire employees, and others work with independent contractors (self-employment). Each status has its pros and cons. To learn more, Google "employee vs. independent contractor."

◆ Call centers whose applications include credit or background checks may require applicants to cover the fees.

◆ As noted earlier, some call centers require that independent contractors pay for training. This does not mean the company is illegitimate or shady, provided, of course, the training cost is reasonable. (We have made an effort to eliminate any company with unreasonable training costs.) The company is simply complying with IRS regulations that determine independent contractor status.

Searches you may want to try:

◆ "call center" + "work from home"
◆ "customer service" + "call center" + home
◆ "customer care" + "from home"
◆ "customer service" + "work at home"
◆ CSR + "at home"

Insider Tip

Mary Naylor, CEO and cofounder, VIPdesk:

"The first thing that we look for in a Home-based Customer Care Representative is superb customer service skills. We look for candidates who desire to serve, are customer focused, have an excellent tone of service, are resourceful and able to troubleshoot challenges."

1-800-FLOWERS *Authors' note: Some positions may be seasonal, for holiday rush periods, when you may have to work long hours. If holidays are already a hectic time for you, these positions may not be the best fit.*	1800flowers.com	
	Site type:	Direct hire.
	How to use:	View posted positions. The employment page can be a bit long, so try using CTRL+F and search for the word "home."
	Positions/work:	Customer service, sales.
	In their words:	"For more than 30 years, 1-800-FLOWERS.COM, Inc. has been providing customers around the world with the freshest flowers and finest selection of plants, gift baskets, gourmet foods, confections and plush stuffed animals perfect for every occasion."

ACD Direct *Authors' note: This company works on national PBS accounts. Work may be seasonal. Independent contractor positions.*	acddirect.com	
	Site type:	Direct hire.
	How to use:	View posted positions.
	Positions/work:	Customer service.
	In their words:	"You are paid for each minute of talk time, with some incentives. The more you work, the more you earn. And...you decide when to work in the comfort of your own home."

Alpine Access	alpineaccess.com	
Authors' note: Hirer has an excellent reputation, with many home-based workers reporting that they love their jobs. *Fee for background check.*	Site type:	Direct hire.
	How to use:	View posted positions.
	Positions/work:	Customer care.
	In their words:	"In 1998 Alpine Access pioneered a simple, yet revolutionary approach to customer care: Rather than bring the people to the work, bring the work to the people. By hiring home-based agents Alpine Access has the most qualified, mature, and experienced customer care professionals in the industry."

Arise	arise.com	
Authors' note: Hirer has an excellent reputation, and many satisfied workers (contractors). *Fee for background check and training.*	Site type:	Direct hire.
	How to use:	View posted positions.
	Positions/work:	Customer service.
	In their words:	"Arise has made a habit out of breaking new ground. From our inception 10 years ago as Willow CSN, innovation has been a key component of our DNA. Our unmatched team has been constructing new ways for people, technology and information to come together to deliver breakthrough results for the customers of America's premier brands."

ARO	callcenteroptions.com	
	Site type:	Direct hire.
	How to use:	View posted positions.
	Positions/work:	Customer service, sales, premium auditors, B2B marketing.
	In their words:	"Our clients are pleased with our highly qualified, motivated, and well-trained staff. Employees are able to work and train from the comfort of their own homes."
Associated Order Processors *Authors' note: Formerly Finger Lakes Web Answering.*	associatedorderprocessors.com	
	Site type:	Direct hire.
	How to use:	View posted positions.
	Positions/work:	Customer service, sales.
	In their words:	"Our training has changed a lot over the last few months, which is why our interview process has become more challenging. We are looking for people that will be with us for a long time, that are dedicated, and willing to be challenged. Our training will last for several weeks. It includes sales training, computer training on our systems, and taking live customer calls."

Cloud 10	cloud10corp.com	
Authors' note: Usually hires employees, but also works with independent contractors for short-term or limited-time projects.	Site type:	Direct hire.
	How to use:	View posted positions.
	Positions/work:	Customer service.
	In their words:	"Cloud 10 utilizes At Home Professionals coupled with leading edge technology and one of the industry's most experienced management teams to provide market leading contact center solutions."

Convergys	convergysworkathome.com	
Authors' note: We know of many people who are happy working for this company.	Site type:	Direct hire.
	How to use:	View posted positions.
	Positions/work:	Customer service.
	In their words:	"As a Convergys Home Agent, you'll interact with customers of leading companies. You may answer questions, determine product opportunities that best meet your callers' needs, place orders on their behalf, provide technical support, or enroll callers in health or entertainment plans."

Hilton	hrccjobs.com	
Authors' note: Hires primarily in Texas and Florida, but we've heard there may be plans to expand into other areas.	Site type:	Direct hire.
	How to use:	View posted positions.
	Positions/work:	Customer service, reservations, sales.
	In their words:	"If you are looking for an environment where you are appreciated, Hilton Reservations Customer Care can deliver. As one of the world's largest hotel chains, we put our people first and are committed to hiring the best. Our company is still growing!"
HSN—Home Shopping Network	hsn.com	
Authors' note: Hiring only in certain U.S. locations. Check site for details.	Site type:	Direct hire.
	How to use:	View posted positions. Click on "careers" link at the bottom of the home page, then on "open positions search engine"; agree to terms; search by field for "customer care/service."
	Positions/work:	Customer service, sales.
	In their words:	"Regardless of the location, HSN employees have several traits in common: passion, energy, creativity, and dedication. We pride ourselves on the community we've built and the services and benefits we offer our team."

LiveOps	liveops.com	
Authors' note:	Site type:	Direct hire.
Hires independent	How to use:	View posted positions.
contractors.	Positions/work:	Customer service.
Excellent reputation. *Highly innovative company.* *Fee for background and credit check.*	In their words:	"LiveOps is leading the revolution in distributed and work from home, agent-based services. We have built the largest network of independent distributed agents in the nation, and we are serious about creating a real business opportunity."

N.E.W. Customer Service Companies, Inc. (*NEW*)	newhomebasedccr.com	
	Site type:	Direct hire.
	How to use:	View posted positions.
	Positions/work:	Customer service.
	In their words:	"*NEW* is the nation's leading provider of extended service plans and buyer protection programs. We deliver outstanding customer care on behalf of the nation's leading retailers, manufacturers, utilities and financial service companies."

Sutherland Global Services	sutherlandathome.com	
	Site type:	Direct hire.
	How to use:	View posted positions.
	Positions/work:	Customer care, technical. support, licensed property and casualty sales, life and health sales.
	In their words:	"Many companies who offer Work from Home employment require that you become a sub-contractor or otherwise known as a '1099 employee.' While we feel that this is certainly a worthwhile approach for some people, it doesn't fit in with Sutherland's corporate culture of mentoring and developing those associates that work hard to achieve success and therefore, all Sutherland @ Home associates are direct hire employees that are every bit as much a part of our corporate family as those who sit in Sutherland facilities."

VIPdesk	vipdesk.com	
Authors' note: We've worked closely with VIPdesk over the years. They are an excellent company from the top down. *Also hires virtual concierges (see "In their words").*	Site type:	Direct hire.
	How to use:	View posted positions.
	Positions/work:	Customer service, sales, "Brand Ambassadors."
	In their words:	"A proven premium service provider with 20 years of experience, VIPdesk specializes in delivering Concierge and Virtual Call Center Services for national brand leaders in several industries that include travel, auto, financial services and retail, by providing high-touch, high-tech branded service platforms that deliver real results and real return on investment."

West at Home	westathome.com	
Authors' note: Employee positions with paid training. We've heard from many happy employees.	Site type:	Direct hire.
	How to use:	View posted positions.
	Positions/work:	Customer service.
	In their words:	"A position with a Fortune 1000 company has never been more convenient. Design your own schedule and begin earning great pay within days of applying."

Concierge

Home-based concierges help individuals and organizations with everything from running errands to finding tickets for a special event. In our time-starved world, more people are turning to these "personal assistants" to help them meet growing commitments and reduce stress.

Considerations:

◆ A concierge must be a great listener, and have solid communication and negotiation skills (for those times when it's necessary to "make the impossible possible").

Searches you may want to try:

◆ concierge + "work from home"
◆ "virtual concierge"
◆ concierge + telecommute
◆ "home-based" + concierge

Insider Tip

Katharine C. Giovanni, president and cofounder, Triangle Concierge, Inc. (*www.triangleconcierge.com*); author of *The Concierge Manual* and *Going Above and Beyond*:

"The secret to the concierge industry is this.... You need to be nice to people. Being warm, friendly and approachable is the key to the industry. You also need to be able to do anything for anyone anywhere at any time."

Office Details	officedetails.com	
	Site type:	Direct hire.
	How to use:	View posted positions.
	Positions/work:	Concierge, virtual assistant.
	In their words:	"At Office Details, we are always interested in hearing from dynamic self-motivated individuals seeking to work in the Virtual Assistance and Concierge industry. All work will be completed as an independent contractor via the Internet, e-mail, fax, phone, and other forms of virtual communication."
VIPdesk *Authors' note: VIPdesk, which is well known for its call center work, began in the concierge business. As mentioned previously, a superior company, catering to top-tier clients.*	vipdesk.com	
	Site type:	Direct hire.
	How to use:	View posted positions.
	Positions/work:	Concierge.
	In their words:	"You will be handling telephone calls and e-mails from the customers of our high-profile, blue-chip clients. Typically, customers call or e-mail and their requests generally fall into one of the following categories: Dining, Entertainment, Travel, Sports & Recreation, Tourist & City, Household, and Shopping."

Consultants and subject matter experts

We joke between ourselves that we know a "little bit about a lot of things." If you know a lot (or everything) about something, you may find the perfect work-at-home role sharing that knowledge with others.

Considerations:

◆ Work may be sporadic or project-to-project.

◆ Most consultant work is performed by independent contractors.

Searches you may want to try:

◆ "subject matter expert" + telecommute

◆ consultant + telecommute

◆ consultant + "work from home"

About.com	beaguide.about.com/topics.htm	
Authors' note: If you've searched the Internet, you've probably met About. com. Comprehensive and very well-respected. Owned by the NY Times Co. *Guides earn a guaranteed monthly minimum, plus traffic incentives.* *Wonderful exposure, and expert positioning!*	Site type:	Direct hire.
	How to use:	View posted positions and criteria.
	Positions/ work:	About.com guides.
	In their words:	"All About.com Guides are freelancers who work online and set their own schedules, giving them the flexibility to work at the time that's best for them. There are other advantages, too, including a compensation plan that offers a base monthly payment combined with incentives for pageview growth, support from our highly trained editorial team, and the opportunity to take part in our Guide-focused PR program."

BrainMass	brainmass.com	
	Site type:	Direct hire.
	How to use:	View posted positions.
	Positions/work:	Subject matter experts, homework help.
	In their words:	"Welcome to BrainMass, the global community of graduate-level students, teachers and professionals. Offering 24/7 expert academic homework help, we are helping students around the world across 45 fields of study."
Clarity Consultants	clarityconsultants.com	
	Site type:	Direct hire.
	How to use:	View posted positions.
	Positions/work:	Subject matter experts; see "In their words," following.
	In their words:	"[I]f you're the best in your field in eLearning, Project Management, Organizational Development, Instructional Design, Leadership Training, SAP Training or in the many other services we provide, we may have a job for you."

HireMinds	hireminds.com	
	Site type:	Search firm.
	How to use:	View listings on site. No keyword search feature, so you'll need to review each listing individually to see if there is a telecommuting option.
	Positions/work:	Subject matter experts, various.
	In their words:	"HireMinds is the leading professional and executive search firm in the Boston area focusing on Biotech/Scientific, Marketing, Technology, Creative, and Administrative roles."

Thesis and Dissertation Advisors On Call	dissertationadvisors.com	
	Site type:	Direct hire.
	How to use:	View posted positions.
	Positions/work:	Freelance thesis and dissertation consultants, APA editors (format experts), A Editors (format experts), statisticians (esp. SAS, Stata, Statistica, Matlab).
	In their words:	"This is NOT a paper mill. Advisors assist students using the same ethical guidelines as faculty advisors. You may not do the student's work (e.g., data collection, ghostwriting). Consultants in high-volume categories (e.g., psychology, education) must be full-time freelancers (i.e., retired from full-time teaching/no 'day job'). We want our students to have your full attention. Priority given to candidates who intend to commit long-term."

Courthouse researchers

Courthouse researchers work "from" home as opposed to "at" home. That is, although you may compile your data at home, you must travel to the local courthouse to gather it. That said, the schedule can be very flexible (during courthouse operating hours), making this a great option in particular for parents who need to work around children's schedules, appointments, and so forth.

Considerations:

◆ Workflow can vary greatly, depending on the county or counties you cover. Generally, the larger the county, the busier you'll be.

◆   Some hirers require no experience, which may be a
    good entry-level option for those with strong research
    and typing skills.

◆   A laptop computer will make this work much easier,
    but computers with a built-in webcam may not be per-
    mitted in some courthouses.

Searches you may want to try:

◆   "court researcher" + "work from home"

◆   "courthouse researcher" + "work from home"

◆   "record researcher" + "work from home"

Accurate Background	accuratebackground.com	
	Site type:	Direct hire.
	How to use:	View posted positions. Employment link is on the "contact" page.
	Positions/work:	Courthouse research.
	In their words:	"Acknowledging Accurate Background, Inc. as an industry leader, U.S. and multi-national organizations trust our customized background screening solutions."

Advanced Background Check	abcheck.com	
	Site type:	Direct hire.
	How to use:	View posted positions.
	Positions/work:	Courthouse research.
	In their words:	"ABC is a full service research and document retrieval firm employing a full staff of experienced researchers in the following fields: mortgage/deed retrieval, current property ownership, UCC filings/searches, credit reports, judgments, bankruptcy, state/federal tax liens and MVR searches."
Jellybean Services *Authors' note: For Canadian readers, note that the company is "expanding into Canada...."*	work4jbs.com	
	Site type:	Direct hire.
	How to use:	View posted positions.
	Positions/work:	Courthouse research, telemarketing, insurance agents, judgment recovery.
	In their words:	"We currently hire independent contractors to perform various tasks for us across the country. In 2009, we are expanding into Canada and hope to have all of Canada serviced by the end of the year. We specialize in court research, but our interests don't stop there."

Judge Mathis (TV program)	judgemathistv.warnerbros.com	
	Site type:	Direct hire.
	How to use:	View posted positions.
	Positions/work:	Courthouse research.
	In their words:	"Judge Mathis is looking for court researchers all across the country [U.S.]."
Sunlark Research	sunlarkresearch.com	
	Site type:	Direct hire.
	How to use:	View posted positions.
	Positions/work:	Courthouse research.
	In their words:	"There are many types of court researchers gathering various information from the public records available. If being your own boss, good earning potential and flexible hours appeal to you, then you may want to consider working as an independent researcher with Sunlark Research."

Education, teaching, and tutoring

The education sector has been quick to incorporate technology generally and the Internet in particular into the way it teaches students and handles work. Most people are aware of the growth in online college courses, but less publicized has been the trend toward virtual teaching in public school systems. (We expect both trends to grow.)

Here, we've listed a variety of home-based jobs such as teaching, tutoring, and test scoring.

As they're so numerous and generally well-known, we haven't listed the online and conventional colleges and universities who hire online instructors (for example, the University of Phoenix, Walden, Capella, Kaplan University, the University of Maryland, and so many more), but they're easy to find with the right search phrases.

Otherwise, visit the Websites of the institutions where you'd like to teach, and check their job openings, which in general are easy to find. You can also try the search terms listed here, which for us have proved quite effective.

Considerations:

◆ Must be comfortable with technology, as you will interface with students in an online environment.

Searches you may want to try:

◆ "online faculty" + position

◆ "online tutor"

◆ instructor + "work from home"

◆ online + tutor

◆ professor + online

Insider Tip

Christa Ehmann Powers, PhD, vice president, Education, Smarthinking, Inc.:

"In light of rapid advancements in computing and communication, working from home as an online tutor is a viable and sustainable alternative to traditional face-to-face educational arrangements. SMARTHINKING tutors work virtually with a variety of students, including high school students, college/university students, and adults in private industry. Grouped according to their area of expertise, tutors and students address a variety of academic issues and projects in both synchronous and asynchronous whiteboard settings; writing tutors also critique essays and written reports. Given the high standards set for SMARTHINKING tutors and the comprehensive discipline specific departments within our virtual work environment, tutors also develop meaningful community with their online colleagues."

Admissions Consultants	admissionsconsultants.com	
	Site type:	Direct hire.
	How to use:	View posted positions.
	Positions/work:	Admissions consultants.
	In their words:	"AdmissionsConsultants continues to grow and we are looking for talented, dedicated, and detail-oriented individuals. If you possess admissions committee experience and excellent interpersonal skills, then we'd like to speak with you about a consultant position."

Berlitz	berlitz.com	
	Site type:	Direct hire.
	How to use:	View posted positions.
	Positions/work:	Language teacher.
	In their words:	"Berlitz International Inc. is the world's premier language services firm, providing expertise in language instruction and cross-cultural training throughout the world. Berlitz has been teaching languages for 130 years and has millions of successful alumni."

The Chronicle of Higher Education	chronicle.com/jobs	
	Site type:	Niche site with job listings.
	How to use:	Use the job search feature. Try search terms such as telecommute, telecommuting, online, virtual, offsite, and remote.
	Positions/work:	Teaching, administrative, managerial.
	In their words:	"The Chronicle of Higher Education is the No. 1 source of news, information, and jobs for college and university faculty members and administrators."
Connections Academy	connectionsacademy.com	
	Site type:	Direct hire.
	How to use:	View posted positions.
	Positions/work:	Teaching.
	In their words:	"Connections Academy, a 'school without walls,' is a virtual educational program serving K–12 students throughout various states in a non-classroom-based environment."

EducateOnline	educate-online-tutoring.com	
	Site type:	Direct hire.
	How to use:	View posted positions.
	Positions/work:	Instructors, technical support, customer support.
	In their words:	"Our unique diagnostic-prescriptive instruction is delivered live, online, to students who are struggling in a specific subject or concept. We work with families at no charge via No Child Left Behind, through academic intervention programs at the school and district levels, and through partners such as Sylvan Learning Center."

Educational Testing Service (ETS)	ets.org	
	Site type:	Direct hire.
	How to use:	View posted positions.
	Positions/work:	Scoring tests.
	In their words:	"Founded in 1947, ETS develops, administers and scores more than 50 million tests annually—including the TOEFL® and TOEIC® tests, the GRE® General and Subject Tests and The Praxis Series™ assessments—in more than 180 countries, and at over 9,000 locations worldwide."

EduwizardS	eduwizards.com	
	Site type:	Direct hire.
	How to use:	View posted positions.
	Positions/work:	Tutoring.
	In their words:	"To tutor at EduwizardS you need a Bachelor's degree or higher. You must have a reliable broadband connection and a headset with microphone. Your knowledge of the subject must be thorough and you should plan to teach only the subject(s) you know best."

Idapted	idapted.com	
Authors' note: We've had a great deal of positive feedback from Idapted Instructors, who love the work and the opportunity to interact with people from around the world.	Site type:	Direct hire.
	How to use:	View posted positions.
	Positions/work:	Conversing with people who are learning English as a second language.
	In their words:	"As an Idapted Instructor you will help students from around the world access better opportunities through improving their English. Our system, content, and training will enable you to be an effective online language instructor and truly have an impact on students' lives."

Nimblemind	nimblemind.com	
	Site type:	Direct hire.
	How to use:	View posted positions.
	Positions/work:	Instructors for adults.
	In their words:	"If you are the best of the best in your field and you have a burning desire to share your specialized knowledge with committed learners from across the globe, Nimblemind would like to talk with you."

NRGbridge. com Online Tutoring	nrgbridge.com	
	Site type:	Direct hire.
	How to use:	View posted positions.
	Positions/ work:	Tutoring grades 4–12, college, SAT, and ESL.
	In their words:	"Do you love teaching? If you are working toward or hold a bachelor's degree or above, we invite you to fill out our online application to tutor for NRG Bridge."

Pearson Education Management	pearsonedmeasurement.com	
	Site type:	Direct hire.
	How to use:	View posted positions.
	Positions/work:	Scoring tests.
	In their words:	"The Educational Measurement group of Pearson is hiring professional scorers to score college entrance exam essays, K–9 writing, reading and math responses."

Smarthinking	smarthinking.com	
Authors' *note: If you're outside the United States, note the mention that candidates can work from anywhere with Net access.*	Site type:	Direct hire
	How to use:	View posted positions.
	Positions/work:	Tutoring
	In their words:	"The major responsibility is tutoring students of varying abilities and ages; however, responsibilities may include assisting in the training and mentoring of new tutors. Candidates can work from any place where they have computer and Internet access."

Tutor.com	tutor.com	
	Site type:	Direct hire.
	How to use:	View posted positions.
	Positions/work:	Tutoring.
	In their words:	"Earn extra income while helping a student ace an algebra exam [or understand] *Moby Dick*, or providing geometry homework help right from your home computer. Online tutoring offers a rewarding, challenging and fun work-from-home opportunity that allows you to schedule your own hours each week, since the service is available 24/7."

Healthcare

Not so long ago, it would have been hard to believe that any kind of healthcare could be provided where there was no patient. Now, however, triage nurses are working telephonically, home-based radiologists are reading x-ray images sent digitally, physicians are reviewing each other's work online, and even pharmacists are working from home. To quote the Grateful Dead (an ironic reference in the medical section), "What a long, strange trip it's been." And what interesting work-at-home jobs it's led to!

Considerations:

◆ Typically, jobs in healthcare professions require specialized education or experience, making entry-level positions more difficult to find.

Searches you may want to try:

◆ "telephonic triage" + job

◆ telephonic + nurse

◆ telecommuting + pharmacist

◆ teleradiology

◆ "work from home" + pharmacist

Doctors On Demand	docond.com	
	Site type:	Direct hire.
	How to use:	View posted positions.
	Positions/work:	Medical doctor, telemedicine.
	In their words:	"Our physicians can work from anywhere in the world but must be licensed in at least one U.S. state. To become a Doctors on Demand physician, each doctor must undergo a thorough verification process."

FONEMED	fonemed.com	
	Site type:	Direct hire.
	How to use:	View posted positions.
	Positions/work:	RN, telephonic triage.
	In their words:	"FONEMED's Registered Nurses provide telephone triage and health advice to callers across North America. We use computerized Schmitt/Thompson triage guidelines to assist in assessing patients' symptoms."
Imaging On Call	imagingoncall.net	
	Site type:	Direct hire.
	How to use:	View posted positions.
	Positions/work:	Radiologist, teleradiology.
	In their words:	"Teleradiology is a booming industry and one of the fastest-growing areas in healthcare services. The rise in demand for imaging procedures far surpasses the number of radiologists available to interpret them and creates a strong market for teleradiology services and excellent job opportunities for qualified radiologists seeking a career in teleradiology."

McKesson	mckesson.com	
	Site type:	Industry-specific job board.
	How to use:	View posted positions. Use the "advanced search" feature. "Please note: Remote and 'work from home' positions will be listed with no city and state. To search for remote or 'work from home' positions, leave the city and state blank in your search."
	Positions/work:	Various healthcare.
	In their words:	"When you join McKesson you can play an important role in the evolution of healthcare. We're a pioneer in the delivery of supply, health, and information technology solutions across the continuum of care."

Medzilla	medzilla.com	
	Site type:	Job board.
	How to use:	In the "advanced search" feature, search for the "exact phrase": "work from home," "telecommuting position," telephonic, virtual, online, "work at home."
	Positions/work:	Various healthcare.
	In their words:	"Job board and Salary Survey for Biotechnology Career, Medical Career or Science jobs. Serving the pharmaceutical, Biotechnology, Science and Healthcare industries."

Permedion	hmspermedion.com	
	Site type:	Direct hire.
	How to use:	View posted positions.
	Positions/work:	Physician reviewer.
	In their words:	"We seek qualified physicians of every specialty to be part of our Independent Medical Review panel. Requirements to join our panel include appropriate licensure, board certification in specialty, and at least five years of active practice in your specialty in the United States."
UnitedHealth Group *Authors' note: Over the years, the UnitedHealth Group family of companies has been one of the most consistent Fortune 500 hirers of home-based workers.*	careers.unitedhealthgroup.com	
	Site type:	Direct hire.
	How to use:	View posted positions using job search. Try the keywords: telecommute, telecommuting, "work from home."
	Positions/work:	Various.
	In their words:	"UnitedHealth Group is a diversified health and well-being company dedicated to helping people live healthier lives. UnitedHealth Group serves more than 73 million individuals worldwide."

Virtual Radiologic	virtualrad.net	
	Site type:	Direct hire.
	How to use:	View posted positions.
	Positions/work:	Teleradiologist.
	In their words:	"Virtual Radiologic is a leading provider of teleradiology services and solutions. We are operated by a unique blend of world-class radiologists and proven business professionals in a unified team environment."

Human resources

Whereas some HR professionals work for companies that are still trying to get their minds around telework, others are more fortunate. HR-related jobs making their way home include generalists, managers, directors, resume writers, recruiters, training-curriculum developers, and more.

Considerations:

◆   Entry-level, work-at-home HR positions can be hard to find, as many companies prefer their HR people to gain on-site experience before teleworking.

Searches you may want to try:

◆   virtual + recruiter

◆   "HR manager" + "work from home"

◆   recruiter + "work from home"

◆   "resume writer" + freelance

◆   "human resources" + telecommuting

◆   "resume screener" + "work from home"

◆   "work from home" + "human resources"

◆   telecommute + "human resources"

Enid, Chesterfield & Company	enidchesterfield.com	
	Site type:	Direct hire.
	How to use:	View posted positions.
	Positions/work:	Recruiters.
	In their words:	"Our greatest assets are the relationships that our consultants have built. We work in a collaborative environment where teaming and networking are stressed."
ERE	ere.net	
	Site type:	Industry-specific job board.
	How to use:	View posted positions.
	Positions/work:	Recruiting, sourcing, business development, managers, various HR-related posts.
	In their words:	"What began as a discussion forum with a few hundred people has since flourished into the premier online community for recruiters, with more than 95,000 unique visitors per month."

ResumeEdge	resumeedge.com	
	Site type:	Direct hire.
	How to use:	View posted positions.
	Positions/work:	Resume writers.
	In their words:	"ResumeEdge's hand-picked team of Resume Writers specializes in 40 different industries to provide the highest quality resume and cover letter services available, bar none. ResumeEdge provides a variety of professional resume services that can help you land your dream job."

Legal

For some time now, solo practitioners have often realized the benefits of working from a home office. Now, thanks in part to the work/life balance movement, we're seeing larger firms dip toes in the water, gradually permitting their attorneys and paralegals to telecommute. (Though rare, some firms are even entirely virtual.)

In the government sector, attorneys in the United States are making some telework progress—at least in the Patent and Trademark Office—though back in the private sector there's a new "lawyer on virtual tap" option, too, for attorneys looking to work gig-to-gig.

The jury is still out, however, on the career consequences in conventional firms of absenting oneself "too often" from the main office. Perhaps the texting generation will bring broader perspectives.

Considerations:

◆ Most teleworking attorney positions will require that applicants be licensed to practice in a specific state or states.

Searches you may want to try:

◆ telecommute + attorney

◆ telecommuting + attorney

◆ "home-based" + lawyer

◆ paralegal + "work from home"

Counsel On Call	counseloncall.com	
	Site type:	Industry-specific job board.
	How to use:	View posted positions.
	Positions/work:	Attorney, paralegal.
	In their words:	"Counsel On Call Attorneys have earned the ability to control when, where and how they work—whether it's 10 or 70 hours per week. We provide opportunities with the nation's leading corporate legal departments and law firms that offer a refreshing level of work-life balance for talented attorneys."
E.P. Dine Inc. *Authors' note: This search firm periodically posts positions for telecommuting or home-based attorneys.*	epdine.com	
	Site type:	Industry-specific search firm.
	How to use:	View posted positions.
	Positions/work:	Attorneys.
	In their words:	"In legal placement there is one name: E.P. Dine Inc. Exceeding client expectations in placement since 1975, our firm is uniquely qualified to deliver precisely the attorney required for every client need. Indeed, for many law firms and corporations, we are not simply the best placement source—we are the only source."

E-Typist Transcription	e-typist.com	
	Site type:	Direct hire.
	How to use:	View posted positions.
	Positions/work:	Legal transcription.
	In their words:	"E-Typist transcriptionists have the flexibility of scheduling their own hours to fit their lifestyles, and work around career and family demands. We require excellent skills and high quality work product of our team members, and consider only applicants with a minimum of three years' legal transcription experience...."

HIRECounsel	hirecounsel.com	
	Site type:	Industry-specific search firm.
	How to use:	View posted positions.
	Positions/work:	Attorneys.
	In their words:	"When you need the finest temporary legal staff, dedicated service, and space management, as well as technology, HIRECounsel is the answer."

MicroMash	micromashbar.com	
	Site type:	Direct hire.
	How to use:	View posted positions.
	Positions/ work:	Bar exam mentor.
	In their words:	"Our unparalleled Mentor Program pairs you with an attorney-mentor who provides you with personalized feedback on your essay assignments and offers general guidance throughout the exam preparation process."

Medical transcription

Medical transcriptionists, or "MTs," type dictated medical notes and records from voice recordings made by physicians or other healthcare professionals. This and other health-related fields are expected to thrive as 70M+ Baby Boomers reach their senior years.

Considerations:

◆ MTs often use a foot pedal and headset. In some cases, special software may also be required.

◆ A quiet environment is essential, as the work demands focus and attention to detail.

◆ MT work is usually deadline-driven, and hence offers flexibility for those who need or prefer nontraditional work hours.

◆ Training is usually required, and most companies test applicants before hiring.

◆ Many community colleges offer medical transcription courses, and home study options are available as well.

Searches you may want to try:

◆ "medical transcription" + "work from home"

◆ "medical transcriptionist" + "home-based"

◆ "medical transcription" + "acute care" + "from home" (change "acute care" to any specialty area)

◆ "entry level" + "medical transcription" + "work from home"

AccuScribe	accuscribe.net	
	Site type:	Direct hire.
	How to use:	View posted positions.
	Positions/work:	Medical transcription.
	In their words:	"AccuScribe leads a team of medical transcriptionists throughout the United States and Canada to transcribe hospital and government records."

Amphion Medical Solutions	amphionmedical.com	
	Site type:	Direct hire.
	How to use:	View posted positions.
	Positions/work:	Medical transcription.
	In their words:	"You can work for a company founded on high billing and payroll ethics and partner with a supportive, communicative management team led by experienced medical language specialists with a passion for quality like no others."

Applied Medical Services	appliedmedicalservices.com	
	Site type:	Direct hire.
	How to use:	View posted positions.
	Positions/work:	Medical transcription.
	In their words:	"For over 25 years Applied Medical Services has worked to establish its excellent reputation and high client satisfaction rating. We know that the key to our ongoing success is our highly skilled team of medical transcript, medical billing and medical coding professionals!"
Ascend Healthcare Systems	ascendhealthcare.com	
	Site type:	Direct hire.
	How to use:	View posted positions.
	Positions/work:	Medical transcription.
	In their words:	"Ascend offers advanced outsource services for clinical documentation, including Transcription and Coding."
ExecuScribe	execuscribe.com	
	Site type:	Direct hire.
	How to use:	View posted positions.
	Positions/work:	Medical transcription.
	In their words:	"We provide high quality medical transcription services 24 hours, 7 days a week. Our team of qualified and experienced medical transcriptionists serves a wide variety of clients including hospitals, clinics and group practices."

MTJobs.com	mtjobs.com	
Authors' note: This site is one of our favorites. We and our Rat Race Rebellion researchers use it regularly with great results.	Site type:	Industry-specific job board.
	How to use:	Use the "Search Jobs!" feature. From the "At home position or at the company" drop-down menu, select "Work from home."
	Positions/work:	Medical transcription.
	In their words:	"[T]he Internet's largest source of medical transcription jobs and resumes. This site is dedicated to medical transcriptionists and medical transcription companies!"

Precyse Solutions	precysesolutions.com	
	Site type:	Direct hire.
	How to use:	View posted positions.
	Positions/work:	Medical transcription.
	In their words:	"Working at Precyse Solutions means being part of a company that views its employees as its most important asset. Precyse is a community of dedicated and experienced professionals providing the highest quality services."

Probity Medical Transcription	probitymt.com	
	Site type:	Direct hire.
	How to use:	View posted positions.
	Positions/work:	Medical transcription.
	In their words:	"Our rapid growth means we are always looking for qualified professionals...like you!"

SoftScript	softscript.com	
	Site type:	Direct hire.
	How to use:	View posted positions.
	Positions/work:	Medical transcription.
	In their words:	"SoftScript's medical transcriptionist and quality assurance staff is recognized among the best in the industry and we consider them our most important asset! The SoftScript team, combined with the latest automated management techniques, continues to attract the most prestigious clients and personnel in the country."

Spheris	spheris.com	
	Site type:	Direct hire.
	How to use:	View posted positions.
	Positions/work:	Medical transcription.
	In their words:	"Spheris is a leading global provider of clinical documentation technology and services to more than 500 health systems, hospitals, and group practices throughout the U.S. Founded by doctors, Spheris solutions address the needs of practitioners, health information directors, IT directors, and administrators."

Merchandising

As with courthouse research, merchandising involves working "from" home as opposed to "at" home. Most of your physical work will be done at local stores, while preparation and reporting will be done at home.

Merchandisers are, in essence, local brand liaisons for companies that display their products in brick-and-mortar stores. As a merchandiser, you may be tasked with checking product placement, restocking shelves, setting up displays and labeling merchandise, and related duties. Typically, this work will take place at retail chain stores such as supermarkets, drug stores, and so forth, and also at specialty stores.

Considerations:

◆ Merchandising jobs are usually independent contractor positions.

◆ Displays must look attractive, so a keen eye for esthetics and organization is a must.

◆ Some positions may involve lifting packages and other material, so be sure to check the job's specifications.

◆ Organizing displays may require bending, short periods on your feet (30 to 90 minutes, for example), and kneeling for lower displays.

◆ For parents, it may be tempting, but you won't be allowed to bring children along on your merchandising stops.

Searches you may want to try:

◆ "independent contractor" + merchandising + job

◆ merchandising + job + "American Greetings" (or other target company [for example, Hallmark, Nintendo, and so on])

Actionlink	actionlink.com	
	Site type:	Direct hire.
	How to use:	View posted positions.
	Positions/work:	Merchandising.
	In their words:	"We're looking for talented, energetic people who will represent vendors by setting up product displays in area retail stores."

At Your Service Marketing	aysm.com	
Authors' note: Hiring in certain regions of the United States only. Be sure to check site for specifics and expansion of hiring areas.	Site type:	Direct hire.
	How to use:	View posted positions.
	Positions/work:	Demonstrator.
	In their words:	"A Professional Demonstrator is a direct one-on-one sales person between the product and the consumer. As a Professional Demonstrator, you are projecting the image of the product being sampled, the company you are working for and the store. A Professional Demonstrator is the key to introducing new products to the consumer and having them become a household name."

Hallmark	hallmark.com	
	Site type:	Direct hire.
	How to use:	View posted positions.
	Positions/work:	Merchandising.
	In their words:	"Some companies make things. Good things, but, you know… things. Hallmark is another kind of company. We play a unique role in defining and expressing friendship and family and love—and we've done it for nearly 100 years."
The Hershey Company	thehersheycompany.com	
	Site type:	Direct hire.
	How to use:	View posted positions using their job search function. Try the search word *merchandising*.
	Positions/work:	Merchandising.
	In their words:	"With revenues of nearly $5 billion and almost 13,000 employees worldwide, the Hershey Company markets such iconic brands as Hershey's, Reese's, Hershey's Kisses, Kit Kat, Twizzlers, and Ice Breakers."

NARMS (National Association of Retail Marketing Services) *Authors' note: NARMS is a longtime favorite of ours. Thousands of jobs in a wide range of locations are posted to the site, and the straightforward search tools make them easy to find.*	narms.com	
	Site type:	Job board.
	How to use:	Use the job search function to search for jobs in your geographical area and preferred job type.
	Positions/work:	Merchandiser, demonstrator, mystery shopper, field event marketers, assemblers, fixture installers.
	In their words:	"NARMS membership is currently 436 companies and includes merchandising service organizations; event marketing, mystery shopping and demonstration companies; professional installation companies; independent food brokers, consumer goods manufacturers, retailers and associates." "JobBank contains a database of positions available in the retail services industry. You can search the current jobs companies have available in a number of categories and locations. The list of jobs is always current."

National In-Store	nis-retail.com	
	Site type:	Direct hire.
	How to use:	View posted positions.
	Positions/work:	Merchandising.
	In their words:	"Our field management staff and store associates are carefully chosen, trained, and continually audited to provide our brand partners with the highest level of execution standards possible."

Retail Merchandising Services	rmservicing.com	
Authors' note: As it mentions, the company serves Target stores exclusively.	Site type:	Direct hire.
	How to use:	View posted positions.
	Positions/work:	Merchandising.
	In their words:	"RMS merchandises exclusively at Target Stores and has been doing so since 1985. With over 700 employees in 47 states, RMS has a Rep within 10 miles of every Target Store nationwide, including all Super Targets."

SPAR Group	sparinc.com	
	Site type:	Direct hire.
	How to use:	View posted positions.
	Positions/work:	Merchandising, store setups, audits, data collection, inventory, fixture installation, display setup.
	In their words:	"SPAR provides in-store merchandising, database and research services to general retail, mass market, drug, and grocery chains. We specialize in the tactics that turn marketing strategies into solid successes for the biggest and best brands in America."

Nonprofit

Many people mistakenly assume that "nonprofit" organizations are big on idealism but small on income, and therefore don't recruit often and can't afford to pay acceptable wages or salaries. Though they may not offer stock options and fat expense accounts, nonprofits as a group earn more than $600 billion annually, and one in 12 Americans—many home-based—is employed by a nonprofit.

Considerations:

◆ Many nonprofits support continuing education for their employees, which can be a great resume-builder.

◆ Nonprofit employees often note that working for a "cause"-driven organization produces an unusually friendly team spirit.

◆ Nonprofit work typically pays less than corresponding work in the private sector, so make sure you find an organization whose cause or mission inspires you.

Searches you may want to try:

◆ nonprofit + position + "work from home"

◆ nonprofit + telecommuting + job

◆ fundraiser + nonprofit + telecommuting

◆ nonprofit + "work at home"

Insider Tip

Steven Joiner, director, Career Transitions Program, Idealist.org:

"Working at home for a nonprofit will likely not be a full-time possibility. Keep in mind that a lot of nonprofits are very collaborative in their work structure so it is often easier for folks to be in the office working together on a given project rather than all working remotely. As well, a lot of nonprofit work involves direct service with an organization's constituents and that obviously needs to be done in person. That said, there are plenty of positions that offer telecommuting options; it just won't be an option every day. For example, my work at Idealist allows me to work on average [one to two] days a week from home, especially when I am writing or researching or even spending a day catching up on e-mails."

Idealist.org	idealist.org	
Authors' note: Over the years, we've found Idealist.org to be the most dependable source of nonprofit jobs. The selection is broad and updated frequently, so we recommend bookmarking the site and making it part of your daily routine.	Site type:	Niche-specific job search site.
	How to use:	Use the search features to seek positions. Try search terms such as freelance, telecommute, telecommuting, home-based, virtual, telework, remote, offsite, anywhere, home.
	Positions/work:	Various jobs in nonprofit organizations.
	In their words:	"Idealist is a project of Action Without Borders, a nonprofit organization founded in 1995 with offices in the United States and Argentina. Idealist is an interactive site where people and organizations can exchange resources and ideas, locate opportunities and supporters, and take steps toward building a world where all people can lead free and dignified lives."

NonprofitOyster. com	nonprofitoyster.com	
	Site type:	Niche-specific job search site.
	How to use:	Use the search features to seek positions. Try search terms such as freelance, telecommute, telecommuting, home-based, virtual, telework, remote, offsite, anywhere, home.
	Positions/work:	Various jobs in nonprofit organizations.
	In their words:	"From personal experience, we believe that employment related to the nonprofit sector is underrated and under-resourced, yet working in and with the nonprofit sector offers great personal fulfillment, spiritual growth, and community bonds."
Philanthropy Northwest	philanthropynw.org	
	Site type:	Niche-specific job search site.
	How to use:	Use the search features to seek positions. Try search terms such as freelance, telecommute, telecommuting, home-based, virtual, telework, remote, offsite, anywhere, home.
	Positions/work:	Various jobs in nonprofit organizations.
	In their words:	"Our job bank has proudly served the Northwest nonprofit community since 1999. We welcome you to this new and improved job bank designed to serve you better."

ReliefWeb	reliefweb.int	
	Site type:	Nonprofit job board.
	How to use:	Use the advanced search feature (start at "professional resources" and click on "vacancies"). Try keywords such as freelance, telecommute, telecommuting, home-based, virtual, telework, remote, offsite, anywhere, home, online.
	Positions/work:	Various jobs in nonprofit organizations.
	In their words:	"ReliefWeb is the world's leading online gateway to information (documents and maps) on humanitarian emergencies and disasters. An independent vehicle of information, designed specifically to assist the international humanitarian community in effective delivery of emergency assistance, it provides timely, reliable, and relevant information as events unfold, while emphasizing the coverage of 'forgotten emergencies' at the same time."

Notary (mobile)

Working as a mobile notary is another from-home as opposed to at-home option, for those who would like to be home-based without feeling home-tethered.

Similar to their traditional counterparts, mobile notaries are public officers who certify or attest to the execution of documents. As a mobile notary, you might be contracted by financial lenders and loan signing companies, for example, to oversee and notarize the signing of mortgage and loan documents.

Mobile notaries became popular when the public began to use the Internet to find lenders, who were often far away. In these "long-distance" transactions, where lenders didn't have a local agent to notarize and oversee documents, mobile notaries filled the gap—and still do.

Considerations:

◆ Notaries are often tested and appointed by their state of residence.

◆ Requirements to become a notary vary by state. Your county or town clerk should be able to provide specifics. National notary associations also post information online. (Google "how to become a notary.")

◆ Filing or application fees to become a notary (usually modest) also vary from state to state. Additional fees may apply.

Searches you may want to try:

◆ "mobile notary" + position

◆ "mobile notary" + [your state here]

◆ "work from home" + notary

◆ "mobile notary" + "independent contractor"

Insider Tip

Greg Evert, Strategic Partnership Manager for American Title, Inc.:

"There is a great need for reliable and cost effective Mobile Notaries, especially in the Settlement Services Industry. In today's technology-driven environment, many people can get approved for a refinance and/or second mortgage without leaving the comfort of their own home. Many lenders want their customers to close on their loan at a time and location that is most convenient for them whether it be at work, home, or even on the golf course. Mobile Notaries are there to make this happen."

24-7 Nationwide Notary Network	24-7nnn.com	
	Site type:	Notary listing service.
	How to use:	Register for jobs.
	Positions/work:	Mobile notary.
	In their words:	"24-7 is always looking for qualified, friendly people to act as independent contractors. We've always had a strong working relationship with our notaries. If you've worked as a notary before and understand the signing requirements of loan documents, then we'll find work for you."
American Title	americantitleinc.com	
	Site type:	Notary listing service.
	How to use:	Register for jobs.
	Positions/work:	Mobile notary.
	In their words:	"We pride ourselves on our Midwestern values and work ethic, which translates into the work we do and the service we provide for the growing real-estate industry. Every one of our 300 (and growing) employees stands strong behind our belief in 'Service Without Boundaries' across this nation, offering unsurpassed customer service every day."

Bancserv	bancserv.net	
	Site type:	Notary listing service.
	How to use:	Register for jobs.
	Positions/work:	Mobile notary.
	In their words:	"Through a network of over 7,500 qualified notaries, we coordinate and simplify the loan closing process by sending notaries directly to a borrower's home or workplace to sign loan documents. This value-added service eases the signing process for both the borrower and lender alike by providing a professional, convenient and flexible signing alternative."
JMT Document Services	documentsigners.com	
	Site type:	Notary listing service.
	How to use:	Register for jobs.
	Positions/work:	Mobile notary.
	In their words:	"Our nationwide network of trained and experienced mobile notaries can deliver your documents to the borrower and help them accurately execute the documents to turn papers into loans."
Notaries To You	notariestoyou.com	
	Site type:	Notary listing service.
	How to use:	Register for jobs.
	Positions/work:	Mobile notary.
	In their words:	"Notaries To You is committed to excellence in every step of the signing process. The scheduling staff are experienced in escrow, title and lending. We are ready to meet any challenge and can get the job done."

Superior Notary, LLC	superiornotary.com	
	Site type:	Notary listing service.
	How to use:	Register for jobs.
	Positions/work:	Mobile notary.
	In their words:	"Superior Notary, LLC is looking for notaries in select areas with loan signing experience. You must have at least 2 years of loan closing experience and average no less than 5 signing[s] per month for the last 3 months to qualify for our prescreening process."

Technical and Web-related

Web and technical jobs were among the first to veer off from brick-and-mortar to virtual arrangements, and the sector continues as one of the beacons and an inspiration to the "distributed workforce" movement.

It makes sense that IT would be at the bleeding edge of telework. After all, these are the people and companies who invented the tools to make virtual work possible. (It also helps that IT often attracts individualists, iconoclasts, mavericks, apple-cart-upsetters, and people who just don't like rules. Who better to hate commuting and having to dress up for the office?)

Considerations:

◆ Technology seems to change daily, at an ever-accelerating pace. Landing and retaining a job in the IT sector, or finding success as a freelancer, will be easier for those who like a whiff of chaos, but also have a firm grasp of the roots from which new ideas sprout.

Searches you may want to try:

◆ "web developer" + job + telecommute

◆ "telecommuting position" + "web designer"

◆ telecommuting + programmer

◆ "work from home" + "technical support"

Accolade Support	accoladesupport.com	
	Site type:	Direct hire.
	How to use:	View posted positions.
	Positions/work:	PC desktop support agents.
	In their words:	"Accolade Support is a rapidly growing division of Tier 3 Support, Inc. We are looking for remote agents to join our team, working from your home office."
Ancient Geek	ancientgeek.com	
	Site type:	Direct hire.
	How to use:	View posted positions.
	Positions/work:	Tech support.
	In their words:	"When other network support companies put you on hold, Ancient Geek puts you first. Our world-class customer service and unique partnership approach are a step above the rest, with proactive, personalized network solutions that minimize downtime and maximize productivity."

Arise	arise.com	
Authors' note: This company has an excellent reputation, and many satisfied contractors. (Also hires customer service reps.)	Site type:	Direct hire.
	How to use:	View posted positions.
	Positions/work:	Technical support.
	In their words:	"If you have a passion about technology and are good at providing solutions, Arise offers you the opportunity to provide service for and support cutting edge Fortune 500 companies from the comfort of your home and be a part of the most rapidly growing segment of the economy."

Art & Logic	artlogic.com	
	Site type:	Direct hire.
	How to use:	View posted positions.
	Positions/work:	Software and design professionals.
	In their words:	"Our geographically distributed business allows us to hire the best developers throughout North America—without requiring them to relocate. We're always looking for exceptional developers to add to our community."

Authentic Jobs	authenticjobs.com	
Authors' note: Another Rat Race Rebellion favorite. This site is easy to scan visually, and routinely posts excellent positions that can be filled from anywhere.	Site type:	Niche-specific job board.
	How to use:	View posted positions. Scan for those that list "anywhere" or "telecommute" in the "location" column. Also try clicking on the "freelance" tab to view independent contractor positions exclusively.
	Positions/work:	Various IT and computer positions, full-time and freelance, with an emphasis on Web design, graphic design, developers, and programmers.
	In their words:	"Since 2005, qualified candidates have been applying for great opportunities at Apple, MSNBC.com, the Motley Fool, Estée Lauder, Turner Sports Interactive, ESPN, Phinney Bischoff, Garmin, Sony BMG, Electronic Arts, HP, and many other companies large and small."

ComputerJobs.com	Computerjobs.com	
	Site type:	Niche-specific job board.
	How to use:	Use the "advanced search" feature for best results. Try search terms such as freelance, telecommute, telecommuting, home-based, virtual, telework, remote, offsite, anywhere, home.
	Positions/work:	Various IT and computer jobs.
	In their words:	"ComputerJobs.com is a leading job board focused solely on the IT professional. Founded in 1995 by IT professionals who saw a need for an effective way for job seekers and companies to connect, ComputerJobs.com has over 13 years' experience connecting thousands of high-tech employers with millions of qualified job seekers."

DevBistro	devbistro.com	
	Site type:	Niche-specific job board.
	How to use:	Check the "telecommute" box in the job search feature, and/or search by keyword with terms such as freelance, telecommute, telecommuting, home-based, virtual, telework, remote, offsite, anywhere, home.
	Positions/work:	Various IT and computer jobs.
	In their words:	"The tech jobs listed here vary from freelance telecommuting projects to full-time jobs and encompass a range of technical skills such as Programming, Web Development, Web Design, Graphic Design, Webmaster, SEO, Software Architecture, Database Administration, Testing/QA, Network and System Administration, Technical Writing, Hardware/Tech Support and related."
Dice *Authors' note: Dice.com is another of our favorites. It consistently turns up excellent tele-commuting IT positions.*	dice.com	
	Site type:	Niche-specific job board.
	How to use:	Use the "advanced search" feature for best results. Try search terms such as freelance, telecommute, telecommuting, home-based, virtual, telework, remote, offsite, anywhere, home.
	Positions/work:	Various IT and computer jobs.
	In their words:	"Dice.com, a Dice Holdings company, is the leading career website for technology and engineering professionals, and the companies that seek to employ them, in the United States."

First Beat Media	firstbeatmedia.com	
	Site type:	Direct hire.
	How to use:	View posted positions.
	Positions/work:	Various IT and computer jobs.
	In their words:	"We are looking to bring aboard motivated individuals who have the same desires and goals we have. All positions will be paid positions and allow the flexibility of working from your home."

FreshWebJobs	freshwebjobs.com	
	Site type:	Niche-specific job board.
	How to use:	View posted positions. Use the search feature with terms such as freelance, telecommute, telecommuting, home-based, virtual, telework, remote, offsite, anywhere, home.
	Positions/work:	Various IT and computer jobs.
	In their words:	"A job board for web pros.... As a registered job seeker you will be able to save and mark job postings on FreshWebJobs."

JustTechJobs	justtechjobs.com	
Authors' note: *This site belongs to WebMediaBrands, which also owns Just Windows Jobs and Just Technology Writer Jobs. Search each site in the same way to turn up even more jobs.*	Site type:	Niche-specific job board.
	How to use:	Use the "advanced search" feature for best results. Try search terms such as freelance, telecommute, telecommuting, home-based, virtual, telework, remote, offsite, anywhere, home.
	Positions/work:	Various IT and computer jobs.
	In their words:	"JustTechJobs.com is Internet.com's jobsite and part of the WebMediaBrands. It provides Employers with a technology-specific focus and provides Job Seekers with job postings aimed at those specific tech jobs. The benefit of using JustTechJobs.com is that it offers a community of 15 million tech professionals supported by 120 tech Websites."

Krop	krop.com	
	Site type:	Niche-specific job board
	How to use:	View posted positions. Use the search feature with terms such as freelance, telecommute, telecommuting, home-based, virtual, telework, remote, offsite, anywhere, home.
	Positions/work:	Web design, graphic design, developers, programmers, and various other IT/creative positions
	In their words:	"Krop is a Job Board and career resource Website for creative professionals. Whether you're looking for a job or hunting top-notch talent, Krop's simple and powerful tools are geared toward connecting the world's brightest minds with the best companies."

MySQL AB	mysql.com	
Authors' note: *MySQL AB is owned by Sun Microsystems, which for years has been on the leading edge of the telework movement. (See more on Sun in Chapter 10.)*	Site type:	Direct hire.
	How to use:	View posted positions. The MySQL jobs link will direct you to the Sun Microsystems job site. Use the search feature with search terms such as freelance, telecommute, telecommuting, home-based, virtual, telework, remote, offsite, anywhere, home.
	Positions/work:	Various IT and computer jobs.
	In their words:	"The corporate culture at Sun is very special. We care about customers, about each other, and about innovation. We want our employees to work well together, make bold decisions and to move fast. We believe that The Network is the Computer."

Transcription (non-medical)

The work in this niche typically involves typing word for word from audio files or other recordings. Companies in most cases seek applicants who have had training. However, some will hire newcomers who can pass their qualification tests.

Considerations:

◆ Companies hiring independent contractors may require that you have your own transcribing equipment (Dictaphone, foot pedal, headset, and so on).

◆ Work may include anything from TV-based recordings to law enforcement tapes, shareholder calls, and so forth. Look for companies offering material that you will find interesting. This will help you stay focused.

Searches you may want to try:

◆ "legal transcription" + "from home"

◆ "legal transcriptionist" + "at home"

- "law enforcement transcription" + "from home"
- "law enforcement transcriptionist" + "at home"
- "financial transcriptionist" + "from home"
- "transcribe meeting minutes" + "at home"

AccuTran Global	accutranglobal.com	
	Site type:	Direct hire.
	How to use:	View posted positions.
	Positions/work:	Transcription.
	In their words:	"AccuTran Global is primarily a financial transcription firm and offers various opportunities for independent contractors around the world. We are one of the few legitimate work-from-home opportunities available."

American High-Tech Transcription & Reporting, Inc. *Authors' note: All applicants must undergo a criminal background check.*	htsteno.com	
	Site type:	Direct hire.
	How to use:	View posted positions.
	Positions/work:	Transcription.
	In their words:	"American High-Tech Transcription & Reporting, Inc., is owned by Susan and Mickey Segal. It was incorporated in 1994 as an expansion of Segal Reporting Services, which was incorporated in 1981."

Fantastic Transcripts	fantastictranscripts.com	
	Site type:	Direct hire.
	How to use:	View posted positions.
	Positions/work:	Transcription.
	In their words:	"For over 10 years, Fantastic Transcripts has been producing fast, accurate transcripts for the business, conference, technical, pharmaceutical and academic worlds."
Morningside Partners	emediamillworks.com	
	Site type:	Direct hire.
	How to use:	View posted positions.
	Positions/work:	Transcription.
	In their words:	"Morningside produces verbatim transcripts of broadcast programming that appears on CNN, FOX News, MSNBC, and CNBC, among other leading broadcast programs. Morningside also produces and distributes other select verbatim transcripts of corporate earnings and shareholder relations events and calls."

Mountain West Processing	mountainwestprocessing.com	
	Site type:	Direct hire.
	How to use:	View posted positions.
	Positions/work:	Transcription.
	In their words:	"We offer a variety of services such as Document Coding, Transcription, and Research. Our independent contractors adhere closely to the requirements of our clients and we offer the highest quality in terms of turn-around time, formatting, and special instructions."

Net Transcripts	nettranscripts.com	
	Site type:	Direct hire.
	How to use:	View posted positions.
	Positions/work:	Transcription, word processing.
	In their words:	"In business since 1988, and located in Tempe, Arizona, Net Transcripts provides secure, Web-based Criminal Justice and Law Enforcement transcription services...."

Purple Shark Transcriptions	thepurpleshark.com	
	Site type:	Direct hire.
	How to use:	View posted positions.
	Positions/work:	Transcription.
	In their words:	"Since 1995, Purple Shark Transcriptions has been providing high-quality transcripts for corporations, authors, journalists, doctoral students and others of interviews, speeches, dictation, audio conferences, Webinars, etc., in a timely and reliable fashion."

SpeakWrite	speak-write.com	
Authors' note: Periodically, this site has an overflow of applicants and declares a moratorium. Check back regularly for openings.	Site type:	Direct hire.
	How to use:	View posted positions.
	Positions/work:	Transcription.
	In their words:	"As an Internet-based transcription service, SpeakWrite knows the importance of timely and accurate transcriptions of your daily work (correspondence, memos, emails, etc)."
Tigerfish	tigerfish.com	
	Site type:	Direct hire.
	How to use:	View posted positions; employment link is on the "contact" page.
	Positions/work:	Transcription.
	In their words:	"Tigerfish has been in business since 1989; in this time we have built a reputation based upon a commitment to excellence and attention to detail."
TypeWrite Word Processing Service	typewp.com	
	Site type:	Direct hire.
	How to use:	View posted positions.
	Positions/work:	Transcription, mostly legal.
	In their words:	"TypeWrite specializes in transcription in the fields of legal, medical, focus groups, scientific, and entertainment. We provide accurate transcription from the popular standard cassette tape, micro-cassette, 4-track to the newest technology, CD-audio and digital transcription."

Ubiqus	ubiqus.com	
	Site type:	Direct hire.
	How to use:	View posted positions.
	Positions/work:	Verbatim Transcriptionist.
	In their words:	"...Ubiqus has grown to become the world's leading meeting services agency, with two offices in the U.S.—New York (NY) and Irvine (CA)—as well as offices around Western Europe: London (U.K.), Madrid (Spain), Waterford (Ireland), Paris, Marseille, Angers and Saint-Nom La Breteche (France)."

Translation and linguistic

Over the years, we've seen tremendous growth in the demand for home-based translators and linguists, as the Internet and other technologies facilitate and accelerate international commerce and other transactions. The work itself may include over-the-phone interpreting, document translation, localization of software or Websites, editing and proofreading, and similar tasks.

Considerations:

◆ Certain positions will require that an interpreter or translator specialize in a given subject or field in addition to the language pair. For example, besides English and Spanish, an expert might need a background in marketing, finance, or law.

◆ For translators, the work is often deadline-driven, so you must be very organized, and able to stay on task.

Searches you may want to try:

◆ "over-the-phone" + translator

◆ "over-the-phone" + interpreter

- ◆ position + freelance + translator
- ◆ interpreter + telecommute
- ◆ translation + "work from home"

Insider Tip

Corrine McKay, author of *How to Succeed as a Freelance Translator*:

"The demand for highly skilled, specialized and business-savvy translators continues to outstrip the supply. It's a great time to enter the industry as long as you're willing to market yourself assertively. Make sure that your knowledge of your source ('from') language is near-native and that you have excellent writing skills in your target ('into') language. Expect to spend six to 12 months marketing yourself before you're spending most of your time working rather than looking for work. Translation is a small industry; get your name out there and network actively with your colleagues online or through professional associations."

Butler Hill Group	butlerhill.com	
	Site type:	Direct hire.
	How to use:	View posted positions.
	Positions/work:	Linguists, software testers, library science and other search experts.
	In their words:	"We recruit and maintain exceptional people using the Free Agent approach. We proudly offer long-term contract positions with maximum flexibility and excellent hourly wages. These positions allow for the ability to work from any location, a flexible workday, and seasonal schedules."

CTS LanguageLink	ctslanguagelink.com	
	Site type:	Direct hire.
	How to use:	View posted positions.
	Positions/work:	Telephonic interpreter, translator.
	In their words:	"At CTS LanguageLink, all of our employees are aligned around a common vision: to provide trusted multilingual communications that speak your customer's language."

Idapted	idapted.com	
Authors' note: We've heard very positive feedback from Idapted Instructors, who love the work and the opportunity to interact with people from around the world. No teaching experience required.	Site type:	Direct hire.
	How to use:	View posted positions.
	Positions/work:	Conversing with people who are learning English as a second language.
	In their words:	"As an Idapted Instructor you will help students from around the world access better opportunities through improving their English. Our system, content, and training will enable you to be an effective online language instructor and truly have an impact on students' lives."

LanguageLine Services	languageline.com	
	Site type:	Direct hire.
Authors' note: *A Rat Race Rebellion favorite,* LanguageLine *regularly posts home-based positions for many language pairs.*	How to use:	View posted positions.
	Positions/work:	Over-the-phone interpreter.
	In their words:	"As the need to communicate with immigrants from all corners of the world grows, thousands of businesses and services turn to over-the-phone interpretation every day to overcome the language barriers between themselves and their limited English-speaking customers, patients, and citizens."

The LINGUIST List	linguistlist.org	
	Site type:	Niche-specific job board.
Authors' note: *We often find great academic and corporate telecommuting positions on this board.*	How to use:	Use the job search feature with keywords such as telecommute, telecommuting, freelance, anywhere, online, home.
	Positions/work:	Various translation and linguistic positions.
	In their words:	"The LINGUIST List is your premier source for information on academic and professional positions for linguists."

Lionbridge Technologies	lionbridge.com	
Authors' note: In addition to translation and interpretation positions, Lionbridge often posts home-based positions that reach beyond the expected. Be sure to check their careers page often.	Site type:	Direct hire.
	How to use:	View posted positions.
	Positions/work:	Freelance translators and interpreters, Internet judges.
	In their words:	"At Lionbridge, we pride ourselves on our network of people. Great people work for us as employees, as translators, and as interpreters. Our more than 4,500 people across 26 countries are supported by thousands more who enable our clients' global success. We are always recruiting the best to work with us in all capacities."

Rosetta Stone	applicants.rosettastone.com	
	Site type:	Direct hire.
	How to use:	View posted positions.
	Positions/work:	Teaching online language classes; see main site at RosettaStone.com for other positions.
	In their words:	"Rosetta Stone recruits the best people. We're a nexus of brilliance, attracting talent from the worlds of programming, language development, education, marketing, advertising, and more. And we're bringing language-learning success to every corner of the globe."

TELELANGUAGE	telelanguage.com	
	Site type:	Direct hire.
	How to use:	View posted positions.
	Positions/work:	Telephonic interpretation.
	In their words:	"TELELANGUAGE allows you to choose your own working hours and provides you the best opportunity for a flexible and fulfilling career. Choosing to work for TELELANGUAGE means you are choosing the lifestyle you want."
Translators Café	translatorscafe.com	
	Site type:	Message forum with job posts.
	How to use:	View positions posted to the translation job board.
	Positions/work:	Translation and other linguistic services.
	In their words:	"Visitors to TranslatorsCafe .com will find a new and very convenient way to connect with others in the international linguistic community. Apply for work with registered translation agencies. Access useful linguistic news and resources. Or chat with other linguists about issues of the day."

Ubiqus	ubiqus.com	
	Site type:	Direct hire.
	How to use:	View posted positions.
	Positions/work:	Foreign language transcriptionist, interpreter, summary writer, translator, and others.
	In their words:	"Ubiqus pioneered the added value summary document and now has market-leading divisions in the fields of verbatim transcription, foreign language transcription, translation (of both audio and text), interpreting, audience response, audio recording, badges and event software."

Writing, editing, and proofreading

If we're to believe the Hollywood image of writers, they spend long hours cloistered away in shabby little rooms, hunched over the keyboard and snarling at the world, and eventually emerging with a Pulitzer-worthy manuscript.

Although the L.A. version may be open to question, they did get one part right: Many if not most writers prefer to be in their "own space" when they're creating. Hence, writers, editors, and proofreaders are often most content and productive working from home, where they have more control over their environment.

Considerations:

◆ Though hard-copy newspapers and magazines are steadily cutting staff or closing their doors, the Internet still pays for good writing, and burns content at a ferocious clip. You may not get rich, but writers—especially freelancers—are in demand.

Searches you may want to try:

◆ freelance + writer + telecommute

◆ proofreader + "work at home"

◆ telecommuting + "copy editor"
◆ "seeking a freelance" + writer (replace "writer" with your preferred job title)

Note: Although blogging has deservedly received much attention, bloggers rarely earn a full-time income. Accordingly, we cover blogging in Chapter 12.

Associated Content	associatedcontent.com	
	Site type:	Content submission site.
	How to use:	Sign up to become a "source."
	Positions/work:	Writing.
	In their words:	"The amount of money you can make at Associated Content is unlimited. As you generate more page views, your Clout level rises—and your Performance Payments do too! Some Sources treat Associated Content as their primary source of income and live off their earnings, taking home hundreds in Performance Payments each month. There are many others who consider AC to be a great source of supplementary income."
Berkeley Graduate School of Journalism	journalism.berkeley.edu	
	Site type:	Industry-specific job board.
	How to use:	View posted positions.
	Positions/work:	Various writing and related.
	In their words:	"J-Jobs is a service to the journalism community provided by the University of California at Berkeley Graduate School of Journalism."

Freelance Writing	freelancewriting.com	
Authors' note: We especially like their "Morning Coffee" posts, which appear each Tuesday with a nice assortment of writing jobs.	Site type:	Industry-specific job postings, with writer's guidelines.
	How to use:	View posted positions.
	Positions/work:	Writing.
	In their words:	"Freelance Writing Jobs and Articles for Freelance Writers."

Helium	helium.com	
	Site type:	Article posting outlet.
	How to use:	Sign up to begin contributing.
	Positions/work:	Writing.
	In their words:	"Think of Helium as a co-op—we're all stakeholders. We provide the publishing platform and the marketing investment to attract writers, readers and advertisers, while the community—that's you—writes, rates, and moderates the site. For all your efforts, you share in a percentage of Helium's revenue."

JournalismJobs. com	journalismjobs.com	
Authors' note: We visit this site daily in our search for legitimate job leads, and have heard from many writers who found jobs here.	Site type:	Industry-specific job postings.
	How to use:	View posted positions. Select "telecommute" from the drop-down location menu. Try searching with keywords such as telecommute, offsite, telecommuting, freelance, anywhere, online, home.
	Positions/work:	Various writing and related.
	In their words:	"JournalismJobs.com is the largest and most-visited resource for journalism jobs, and receives between 2.5 to 3 million page views a month."

McMurray	jobs.copyeditor.com	
Authors' note: Click on the "ContentWise" link for McMurray's writing and communications job board.	Site type:	Industry-specific job board.
	How to use:	View posted positions. Try searching with keywords such as telecommute, offsite, telecommuting, freelance, anywhere, online, home.
	Positions/work:	Copy editing and related.
	In their words:	"[T]he definitive career resource for *Copy Editor* subscribers and job seekers who are searching for new editorial employment opportunities."

Places for Writers	placesforwriters.com	
	Site type:	Industry-specific job board.
	How to use:	View posted positions.
	Positions/ work:	Various writing and related.
	In their words:	"This is a Canadian writers' resource site. Where possible, we also like to help international writers, too. Since 1997 we have been posting writing contests and submission calls, occasional literary news, publishing information, and links to great Canadian writers and organizations."
ProofreadNOW *Authors' note: This site hires proofreaders in a number of languages.*	proofreadnow.com	
	Site type:	Direct hire.
	How to use:	View posted positions.
	Positions/ work:	Proofreading.
	In their words:	"From simple spelling and grammar mistakes to complicated syntactical errors, our methodology finds everything and points the way toward a much better document."

Sun Oasis	sunoasis.com	
	Site type:	Industry-specific job board.
	How to use:	View posted positions.
	Positions/work:	Various writing and related.
	In their words:	"We aren't just about getting job leads. We want to provide the best job leads! We aren't just about providing a pool of eager job seekers. We are about providing an excellent resource base for those looking for writers, editors, and copywriters."
WritersWeekly	writersweekly.com	
	Site type:	Industry-specific job board.
	How to use:	Click on the "markets" link for a list of paying publishers.
	Positions/work:	Writing.
	In their words:	"WritersWeekly.com is one of the oldest and most respected sites on freelance writing. It has been published continuously since 1997. WritersWeekly.com is part of the Booklocker.com, Inc. family of businesses, which includes epublisher and online book store Booklocker.com."

Companies that hire in more-limited geographical areas

The vast majority of the preceding companies accept applicants from across the United States, and many internationally. However, there are also numerous trustworthy companies that hire home-based workers from a more limited geographical area. We've included a selection of the better-known companies here for readers who live in the specified hiring zones.

Some of these organizations are steadily expanding their recruiting zones. If a company you like isn't hiring in your area now, be sure to check its Website employment pages regularly, so you don't miss a future opportunity.

Company	Link	Type of Work	Location(s)
1-800 Contacts	1800contacts.com	Customer service	Draper, Utah
Affina	affina.com	Customer service	Peoria, Ill. Waterloo, Iowa
American Airlines	aacareers.com	Reservations/ customer service	Cary, N.C. Fort Worth, Texas Tucson, Ariz
Apple	jobs.apple.com	Tech support	Orlando, Fla. Kennesaw, Ga.
Asurion	asurionforceathome .com	Customer service	Evans, Colo. Houston, Texas Nashville, Tenn.
Call Desk	calldesk.com	Customer service	Oregon
Customer Service Review— CSR	csr-net.com	Customer service	Wayne, Pa.
GE Money	gecallcentercareers. com	Customer service	Charlotte, N.C.
Hilton Hotels	hrccjobs.com	Reservations/ customer care	Dallas, Texas Tampa, Fla.

Infocision	infocision.com	Customer service	Ohio West Virginia
JetBlue	jetblue.com	Reservations / customer service	Salt Lake City, Utah
MicahTek	micahtek.com	Customer service	Oklahoma
Palm Coast Data	palmcoastdata.com	Data entry	Palm Coast, Fla.
Prince Market Research	pmresearch.com	Telephone interviewing	Florida Tennessee Texas
Quest Diagnostics	questdiagnostics.com	Tele-interviewer	Lee's Summit, Mont.
Telecare	telcarecorp.com	Telephone survey agent	South Florida

A last suggestion...

As you visit the sites in this chapter and those your own searches uncover, be sure to bookmark those that bear the most fruit or show the most promise. Create a "job search" bookmark folder that you can refer to each time you resume your online search. This will streamline your efforts overall, increase your confidence in your search abilities, minimize the chances of missed leads, and help you navigate quickly to the sites most likely to produce results.

CHAPTER 7

Finding Work-at-Home Jobs on the "Big" Job Boards

When we ask the job seekers in our telework job-finding programs which Websites they're using to find job leads, the majority point to the "big boards"—Monster.com, CareerBuilder.com, HotJobs.com, and craigslist.org. Yet when we explore the various search features and capabilities of those sites, it quickly becomes apparent that most users don't know about, or aren't maximizing, some of their best functions.

Here, we'll take a look at each of these larger sites, share some pointers for "beyond the basics" use, and touch on 25 smaller boards you'll also want to consider.

As you view the job leads themselves, keep in mind that scammers place their ads right alongside those of legitimate companies. Call on your common sense, and the scam-spotting tips from Chapter 4, when you assess these and any other job listings.

As with advertising in other media, the fact that an ad appears on a legitimate Website doesn't mean the ad itself is legitimate.

Monster.com

With millions of unique visitors each month, Monster.com is arguably the world's largest commercial job board. We've watched the site morph throughout the years, improving functions and adding features to enhance the job seeker's overall experience as well as his or her chances of finding exactly what he or she is looking for.

Setting up a Monster.com profile

We suggest you begin by taking advantage of Monster.com's "profile" tool, and assemble a simple but comprehensive profile. This lays the groundwork for a search experience tailored to your background, skills, and objectives. When your profile is done, the Monster home page and other pages will change to display relevant information. For example, the home page will feature a snapshot of your profile, a recommended career path (or relevant career-exploration tool), jobs that match your criteria, and other information to aid you in your search.

If you log in when you visit, Monster.com will load a customized page that lists recommended jobs, tracks your job applications, saves jobs you've indicated an interest in, and archives your saved searches. You can reach this personalized page by clicking on the "jobs" link at the top of the page.

Finally, upload your resume to the Monster.com directory so prospective employers can seek you out, too.

Searching the Monster.com jobs database

If you've come this far with us, you know we're big advocates of "good search phrases" in the hunt for jobs in the popular search engines. The same holds true as we click to the job boards, and the "garbage in, garbage out" principle applies as well. Come to the boards with your best search terms, and you'll get the best results. (Revisit Chapter 5 for more on search terms.)

As with most job boards, Monster's home page presents you with a stripped-down job search interface—one field for keywords, and another for geographic specifications. We suggest you skip the basics and go straight to the "More Search Options" button. Clicking this will open up new fields, and let you perform a highly targeted search.

The expanded search options include:

◆   A checkbox enabling a search for an exact phrase.

◆   A field for words you want to exclude from your search.

◆   A field for entering a company (employer) name.

◆ The ability to specify up to 20 industries (or none, to view jobs in all industries).

◆ A breakdown of hundreds of very specific occupation areas (choose up to 30, or none, to view jobs in all occupations).

◆ "Job Types" (for example, full-time, part-time, per diem, employee, temporary/contract/project, intern, seasonal).

Now let's do a sample search to see how the tools work in action. In this example we'll be hunting for a home-based customer service position with a call center.

At the top of the Monster.com home page, we return to the two basic search fields: one for "keywords" and the other for "location." This is where you begin to put together your job-search parameters.

1. Start by entering one of your best search phrases in the "keyword" field. Let's use the phrase "work from home position" for our test search. *No need for quotation marks, as we'll be using the "exact phrase" option in step 4.*

2. Leave the "location" field blank. *Why limit your geographic choices, when one of the great blessings of telework is the ability to seek jobs and projects with geographically diverse companies?*

3. Click on the "More Search Options" button (below the orange "Search" button") to reveal new search options.

4. Check the box labeled "This exact phrase." *This has the same effect as putting your phrase in quotes, and directs Monster.com's search engine to look for the exact phrase in job descriptions.*

5. As mentioned, you can use the other advanced search options to draw leads from individual companies, or by industry, occupation, or job type. For our test search, we'll simplify and use the "Occupations" option, click on the plus sign by "Customer Support/Client Care," and check off "Call Center."

6. Unleash the Monster. (Click "Search"!)

Now the search engine will scour Monster.com's database of jobs, looking for those "call center" leads that contain the exact phrase "work from home position."

Make a point to experiment with the search tools at Monster.com (and every job board). Test your own variety of search phrases, and add and subtract search options to refine your search and capture every relevant lead.

Whenever a search works well, click the "Save Search" button in the right column to (1) save it to the site for easy reference on future visits, and (2) set up an e-mail alert to have Monster.com send similar leads directly to your e-mail account daily, weekly, bi-weekly, or monthly. It's a wonderful thing to sign in to your e-mail account and find job leads waiting for you!

Monster.com tips and tricks

◆ If you're unsure about your career path, check out the links listed in the "Career Tools" and "Advice" tabs.

◆ The new "Career Mapping" tool is a creative, easy-to-use way to explore a variety of career steps and paths.

◆ If, after posting your resume, you begin to receive unwanted e-mail, change your setting to "Private."

◆ To avoid falling into scams, remember that Monster will never send you an e-mail asking for secure information such as your password, banking data, credit card number, and so forth.

CareerBuilder.com

CareerBuilder.com is owned by Gannett Co., Inc. (the largest U.S. newspaper publisher), Tribune Company, the McClatchy Company, and Microsoft—an impressive roster that helps ensure excellent exposure and brand recognition for this job board.

Its easy-to-use interface, deep database, and quick searches make it a site you'll want to use regularly.

Set up My CareerBuilder

Here, too, we suggest you take a few moments to complete the registration. Once you've done this and your resume is uploaded, CareerBuilder .com's software will assess the keywords in your resume, the jobs you apply for, and the searches you conduct, and generate job recommendations that match your skills and interests.

Your usage history will dictate what appears on your CareerBuilder.com home page, so each time you log in you'll see a list of job recommendations, recently viewed jobs, and other tailored information.

Jump-start with segmented job listings

CareerBuilder.com also provides a great list of "browse by" job categories on the home page. Categories include:

Accounting	Admin & Clerical
Banking & Finance	Business Opportunities
Contract & Freelance	College & Internships
Customer Service	Diversity Opportunities
Engineering	Executive
Franchise	Government
Healthcare	Hospitality
Human Resources	Information Technology
Manufacturing	Nonprofit
Part Time	Retail
Sales & Marketing	Science & Biotech

To search jobs by category, just click on the one you're interested in and you'll either be taken to a sub-page or to a separate site (also owned by CareerBuilder) dedicated to jobs of that kind. For example, the "Contract & Freelance" link leads to Sologig.com—a CareerBuilder.com–owned site developed to connect contractors, freelancers, and so forth, with employers.

Searching the CareerBuilder.com jobs database

When you first arrive at the CareerBuilder.com site, you'll see the same "keyword" and "location" search fields that appear on every popular job board home page. Again, we suggest you move beyond these basic search tools and head right for the advanced options. To access them, just click on the "Find Jobs" link (not the button, but the link) on the upper left side of the page.

Now you'll see an expansive page of options including geographical parameters, job categories, include/exclude criteria, salary range, employment type, date posted, and so on. There's also an option to exclude "non-traditional jobs"—those that require a "fee or investment of money and time to generate income." Unless you're interested in those opportunities, we suggest you check that option for every search, to reduce propositions (including scams) that require payment.

Because there's no "exact phrase" option, you'll need to include quotation marks around any search phrases. (Words alone, of course, require no quotes.)

To see how it works, here's a sample search for a home-based writing position:

1. From the home page, click on the "Find Jobs" link (not the button) toward the top of the page.

2. In the "Keywords" field, we'll use the single word "telecommute." (A number of words or phrases might be effective in our search, but we'll limit ours to "telecommute" to keep things simple. Again, any phrases you use should be enclosed in quotes, to target the precise phrase.)

3. From the first drop-down "Job Categories" menu, select "Media—Journalism—Newspaper." In your own searches, of course, you may choose up to three categories, using all of the drop-downs. To see *all* job listings containing your keyword(s), regardless of category, simply leave the three fields blank.

4. As you'll notice, all "Employment Types" (full-time, part-time, and so forth) are checked off by default. For our search, we'll leave them that way, so we can see all jobs, regardless of "type." If you have a preference, you would indicate it here.

5. Again, to reduce scams and other fee-based propositions, check the box for "Exclude Non-Traditional Jobs."

6. In your own searches, add any other search parameters (for example, salary, degree, excluded criteria, and so on) to optimize your search and results.

7. Click the "Find Jobs" button and review the results.

When you've formulated a search that gives great results, click the "Save this search" link so you can repeat it easily in the future. Also, while setting up your search, you'll have the option to receive e-mail alerts on new job leads. As with other job sites, these can save you time and get you right to the leads. (You can also have job alerts sent via text to your cell phone.) To see these options, just click on the "Job Alerts" link at the top of the page.

CareerBuilder.com tips and tricks

◆ When registering, be sure to uncheck any box that offers to send you e-mail you may not want (offers, job fair alerts, and so forth).

◆ Some offers may pop up during the registration process, and can look very much like a continuation of the registration. To verify, check the top of the page for sponsorship references. If you don't want the offer, click the "No thanks" button at the bottom of the page.

◆ In addition to its jobs database, the CareerBuilder.com site holds a wealth of other information and tools for job seekers. Be sure to click on the "Advice & Resources" link, for example, to find articles and guidance on building your career.

Yahoo! HotJobs.com

One of the first things many users may notice about the HotJobs.com site is its distinctly Yahoo!-ish feel, making Yahoo! lovers feel right at home in this easy-to-navigate environment. In fact, if you already have a Yahoo! account, you can log into HotJobs.com using the same access information.

(If you don't have a Yahoo! account, the sign-up process for HotJobs .com can be a bit more time-consuming than at other boards, as you have to find an available user ID—no small feat with Yahoo!'s popularity—then register an alternate e-mail address, and click on a link in a verification e-mail.)

Searching the HotJobs.com jobs database

As with the previous sites, we suggest you start with the advanced search options. To reach these options, click on the "Job Search" tab at the top of the page, then on the "Advanced Job Search" link on the following page. Your expanded search options will include:

◆ Job Category.

◆ Date Posted.

◆ Experience (years and level).

◆ Education.

◆ Minimum Salary.

- Position Type (full-time, part-time, and so on).
- Travel Amount (from "negligible" up to 100 percent).
- Company Name.
- Company Type.

To take you through the HotJobs.com search process, here's a sample search for a home-based position in human resources.

1. From the HotJobs.com home page, click the "Job Search" tab.
2. On the following page, click on the "Advanced Job Search" link.
3. From the drop-down keywords menu, select "This exact phrase."
4. In the keyword field, enter "home-based" (quotes unnecessary; see above).
5. The "location" field was automatically filled with our own location, so we removed that, and left the field blank in order to conduct a broader search.
6. From the drop-down "Job Category" menu, select "Human Resources."
7. For the "Date Posted," we selected "Within the past 7 days" to assure fresh results.
8. We left the other fields on their default settings, but adjust as necessary to tailor your search to your needs.
9. Click the "Search Jobs" button and review the results.

HotJobs.com tips and tricks

- Visit the "Career Tools" link for articles and other information on interviewing, resumes, salary, networking, and other career development topics.

- HotJobs.com permits you to post multiple resumes, so if you use different resumes to cover several specialties, you can post them all.

- Review the job search tips on the right side of the Advanced Search page for even more search ideas.

craigslist.org

Craigslist.org is the largest classified ad vehicle in the world (sucking air from newspapers internationally), and has become a household name—for good and bad reasons—in recent years. Regardless, the site boasts thousands of jobs on any given day, many of them work-at-home positions.

That said, when we were planning the Rat Race Rebellion site, we decided not to include links to job listings from craigslist.org. That's not to say we don't love the operation; as businesspeople, we salute the innovation, the business model, the growth curve, the whole shebang. It's an awesome achievement. We had three main reasons for our decision:

1. There's an extraordinarily high scam-to-legitimate ratio among the work-at-home job leads posted to craigslist.

2. It sounds self-serving, but we've logged thousands of hours visiting work-at-home Websites and blogs, and we've found that more than 90 percent re-post leads from craigslist.org. There's nothing wrong with this—people do find legitimate leads among the links, and telework deserves to be promoted at every opportunity. But one of our own goals is to offer screened job leads that visitors wouldn't also encounter on hundreds of other sites.

3. Finally, searching craigslist itself for work-at-home jobs is easy, and you can decide for yourself if the leads are good. Here's how.

Finding work-at-home jobs on craigslist.org

Before you begin searching for jobs on craigslist.org, spend some time getting to know the site's layout. One of the first things you'll see is that the content is separated geographically, so you'll need to select a region to get started.

1. Once you've selected your geographical area, move over to the left column and, from the drop-down menu, select "jobs" and click on the ">" button to the right of that menu. You should now find yourself at a listing of jobs that have been posted for the geographical area you selected.

2. To drill down and isolate the telecommuting posts, check the "telecommute" box and click the "search" button.

3. Now you'll have a list of job leads for which the poster has indicated, "telecommuting is OK." (To see what we mean, click on a lead and scroll down to the bottom of the page. In the lower left corner you should see some particulars about the job, among them "telecommuting is OK.")

4. Refine your search by adding keywords and/or selecting a job category from the drop-down menu to the left of the search button.

Remember to check a number of geographical areas. Because these are telecommuting or "virtual" positions, many may be of interest regardless of where you live.

Using Google to search craigslist.org

Just as it scans the content of other sites around the Web, Google sends out its bots (web-robot software) to gather data from the posts made to craigslist.org. This makes Google an excellent tool for finding craigslist.org job leads that have been marked "OK for telecommuting."

To find *all* of the "OK for telecommuting" leads from craigslist.org (be prepared: There will be tens of thousands), simply go to Google and search with the following text:

"telecommuting is OK" + site:craigslist.org

For a more targeted search, however, try these tips:

1. To limit your results to fresher leads, click on Google's "Show options" link. (If you executed the search we just suggested, you'll see the "Show options" link above the results.) Then select the desired time frame: "Recent results," "Past 24 hours," and so forth.

2. Home in on certain types of work-at-home jobs by expanding the search phrase to include a second plus sign and the job type. For example, to find "telecommuting" call center jobs, use this search string:

"telecommuting is OK" + site:craigslist.org + "customer service"

Searching craigslist.org with crazedlist.org

Crazedlist.org (whose slogan is "Search craigslist like a madman") offers another quick path to telecommuting jobs on craigslist.org. Most usefully, the site lets you search across numerous craigslist.org geographic sites at the same time.

In other words, rather than laboriously searching for jobs at the individual craigslist.org sites for Chicago, New York City, and Anchorage, you can use crazedlist.org to check them all (and many more) simultaneously.

To use crazedlist.org:

1. Start at the crazedlist.org home page and check off the geographical area(s) you'd like to search. Or, from the drop-down menu (located just above "AK"), select "all" regions, or "west coast," "northwest," and so on. The states in your chosen region will be checked automatically.

2. From the drop-down "category" menu, select "jobs." This will open option boxes to the right.

3. Check the box for "telecommute," then click on the "Search" button. This will yield all the job listings on craigslist.org that have been marked as "telecommuting is OK."

4. As with the craigslist.org site, you may refine your search by adding keywords and/or selecting a job category. You'll find these on the drop-down menu on the upper left of the page.

Beyond the "biggies": 25 smaller job boards you'll love

A job board doesn't have to be colossal to be effective. In fact, we use a lot of smaller, more targeted boards in our research every day.

Following are some examples of smaller boards that may very well feature just the home-based job or project you want. To make the most of them (we've included some of their highlights), use the search terms and techniques we've covered thus far, and be sure not to miss any relevant pointers on the sites themselves.

Beyond.com	Beyond.com bills itself as the "World's largest network of niche career communities," and it's the "niche" specialization that makes them unique. The site features hundreds of "channels" divided by industry, location, and "specialty," such as: ♦ "The Administrative Channel" ♦ "The Accounting & Finance Channel" ♦ "The Atlanta Channel" ♦ "The Denver Channel" ♦ "The Retirement Channel" ♦ "The Entry Level Channel"
BilingualCareer.com	This site features jobs for bilingual job seekers, and includes many language pairs.
CollegeGrad.com	Developed for college students and recent graduates.
DiversityJobs.com	A job board with a commitment to diversity and companies that embrace pro-diversity hiring practices.
eFinancialCareers.com	A job site for professionals seeking work in the banking and financial sector.
GenuineJobs.com	Registration is free for this site that focuses on telecommuting jobs.
GetTheJob.com	GetTheJob.com gathers job postings directly from the career pages of thousands of companies. As they say on their site, this means "Real Jobs from Real Companies."
GreatInsuranceJobs.com	What can we say that the name doesn't cover?

Hound.com	This site sets itself apart by listing only those jobs posted to company Websites.
	This means you may find jobs not included on the "big boards." And because most scams aren't posted to corporate Websites, it can also dramatically reduce bogus leads.
Job.com	A solid full-service job board with good advanced search options.
JobCentral.com	This board is maintained by the DirectEmployers Association, "a nonprofit consortium of leading U.S. corporations, in alliance with the National Association of State Workforce Agencies."
	Also try Directemployers.jobcentral.com, where their "Advanced" search tools will help you zero in on their leads.
	Remember to use quotation marks around your search phrases at both Websites, as neither has an "exact phrase" search option.
JobFox.com	JobFox establishes a "suitability profile" based on the job seeker's data, then recommends appropriate jobs.
Jobs for PhDs jobs.phds.org	If you have a doctorate and would like to work from home, jobs.phds.org is an excellent resource.
	Focus on the "keywords" field and experiment with terms such as freelance, telecommute, telecommuting, anywhere, offsite, virtual, and remote.
Jobs4HR.com	A good board for jobs in the HR field.
JobsInLogistics.com	Features jobs in logistics and related areas, including supply chain, transportation, freight forwarding, purchasing, sales/ business development, and so forth.
LatPro.com	The first of its kind, LatPro is a job board geared toward bilingual Hispanic job seekers.

Net-Temps.com	Features temporary, temp-to-permanent, and full-time positions posted by staffing agencies.
ProHire.com	Jobs of all kinds in the United States and internationally. Click on a job category, industry, or state, then on the "Modify Search" link to enter keywords.
RetailCareersNow.com	A great job site for retail professionals of all types.
TalentZoo.com	A job site for ad, marketing, and media professionals.
thingamajob.com	Owned by Allegis Group, a staffing company, thingamajob features contract, temp-to-perm, and direct placement jobs.
Trovix.com	Trovix offers a highly personalized approach to job seeking. Their software scans your resume, work experience, and skills, and offers matching job leads.
TweetMyJobs.com	TweetMyJobs.com enables Twitter users to turn the social media platform into a job source.
USAJobs.com	"USAJOBS is the official job site of the U.S. Federal Government. It's your one-stop source for Federal jobs and employment information."
Vault.com	Vault launched as a provider of "insider information and advice" for those pursuing "high-potential" careers. Their job board is easy to navigate and gives fast results.

That's it for job boards large and smaller. But we want to make sure you've got plenty of leads to choose from. So now we'll show you how to find great work-at-home jobs on sites that are leading one of the hottest job-source trends on the Internet.

CHAPTER 8

Finding Home-Based Jobs on Job Aggregator Sites

Job aggregator sites are a fairly new development in the world of online job hunting, and they're catching on like wildfire for their streamlined yet comprehensive approach to job leads.

In a nutshell, a job aggregator site gathers leads from such sources as online recruiters, job boards (Monster, CareerBuilder, and so on) and other Websites, reposts them all in one location, and makes them easy to search.

Benefits of job aggregator sites

Although visiting job boards and conducting a search at each can be effective, it can also be very time-consuming. In "batching the boards," job aggregator sites save you that time. But there are other benefits, too.

◆ **Big fish and small fish in the same pond:** Even if your daily job search includes stops at all the big job boards, you may still miss great leads that have been uploaded to lesser-known sites such as BarefootStudent.com, GoliathJobs.com, TheJobPlanet.com, JobCircle.com, and many more.

◆ **Fresh information:** Aggregator sites are designed to gather job listings from other sites *as they are posted*. You don't have to worry that skipping the individual sites will leave you confined to stale leads.

◆ **Casting a broader net:** Some job aggregator sites such as Indeed.com have a feature that lets you search job leads taken directly from the "career" pages of employer Websites. With the right search techniques, this can quickly put you on the fast track to finding excellent home-based jobs.

◆ **Well-fed job source:** Job aggregator sites accept automated "feeds" from various sources. This brings in job leads unlikely to be picked up by standard job boards, where job ads must be purchased before they are posted.

◆ **Customized searches:** Aggregator sites offer a broad range of search options that allow you to focus your searches by geography, job type, keywords, and other parameters. (Many job boards offer this feature, too, but the search is limited to the individual board.)

◆ **Search agents:** If you're accustomed to using search agents (automated searches that run continuously in the background, using preset search terms) on other job boards, you'll have that option on the aggregator sites as well.

◆ **E-mail alerts:** Some aggregator sites will alert you by e-mail when they post a job matching your criteria. When you use well-considered search terms, this can substantially shorten your hunt for home-based work.

Two leaders in a growing niche

Many good companies are striving to compete in the growing job aggregator niche. As we write, Indeed.com and SimplyHired.com have taken a wide lead.

Here, we'll introduce you to these two aggregator sites, and share some of our best tips for making the most of their resources.

Finding work-at-home jobs on Indeed.com

We use Indeed.com often in our job screening services for the U.S. State Department and other clients (as mentioned, we screen approximately 4,500 to 5,000 leads per week), and we recommend it to our RatRaceRebellion .com job seekers and to our work-at-home seminar participants as well.

With Indeed's significant site traffic (you can check current estimates at Compete.com), it's clear we're not the only ones who consider it a valuable resource.

Indeed, Inc., which is owned in part by the New York Times Company, has this to say about its site:

> *Since 2004, Indeed has given job seekers free access—instantly, in a single search—to millions of jobs from thousands of company websites, job boards, newspapers, blogs and associations. Indeed makes it easy for job seekers to drill down by keyword, location and salary to find exactly the right jobs.*

At the site itself, job seekers find a look and feel similar to other search engines such as Google and Ask.com.

Though many job seekers use the "what" and "where" fields on the entry page to conduct their searches, we recommend you use the advanced features instead, to fine-tune your approach and results. Start by clicking the "Advanced Job Search" link just below the "Find Jobs" button.

The advanced search page unlocks a host of options, including the following:

Search Option	Result
"With all of these words"	Search will return all job postings that contain all of the words entered in this field.
	For example, if you enter the words "work from home" (without the quotes), the search will return all job leads that contain the phrase "work from home," but also all leads containing the individual words "work," "from" and "home" (for example, "If you're <u>from</u> Chicago, and would like to <u>work</u> near your <u>home</u>…").
"With the exact phrase"	We usually recommend this as your default search option. As we mention in more detail in Chapter 5, using well-weighed phrases will yield the greatest number of legitimate leads.
	For example, if you use the phrase "must have a quiet home office" (quotes aren't needed, as the words are already recognized as a fixed phrase), your returns will include only those leads featuring this exact wording (for example, "Agents will handle incoming calls from clients such as QVC and The Shopping Channel. Candidates <u>must have a quiet home office</u>").

"With at least one of these words"	This search option will return job postings that contain any one of the words you enter in the field.
	For example, a search for "work from home" (without quotes) will return all leads that contain the phrase "work from home," but *also* those containing any one of the words (for example, "Nurses must be willing to visit patients at <u>home</u>").
"With none of these words"	Use this field to exclude jobs you don't want.
	For example, if "outbound" phone calling (aka telemarketing) isn't your cup of tea, enter the word "outbound" (no quotes necessary) in this field. All leads that include that word will be omitted from your search results.
	This option can be used in combination with the previous fields. You can search for "home-based agent," for example, while filtering out any ads with the word "outbound." This will help you find customer service positions, handling in-bound calls.
"With these words in the title"	This option allows you to search the job titles or ad headlines for specific words.
	For example, if again you're looking for a customer service position, you might enter the word "customer" in this field. Keep in mind, however, that job titles don't always include the words you might expect, and you may risk excluding good leads from your search.
	This option can also be used in combination with the previous fields. You can search for "work from home," for example, while limiting the results to jobs that include "customer" in the title.
"From this company"	If you're interested in working for a certain company, use this field to find any job leads it may have posted.
	For example, entering "Aetna" in this field will return only those jobs posted by that firm.
	Combining this option with others is also effective. Entering "Aetna" in this field, for example, with the "exact phrase" option set for "work from home," will net jobs from Aetna that contain the phrase "work from home."

"Show jobs of type"	Here, you may select the type of work commitment you are looking for: full-time, part-time, contract, internship, or temporary.
	This field can also be combined with previous fields.
"Show jobs from"	One of our favorites, this field lets you choose to see jobs from "all web sites" (this is the "grab bag" option, pulling leads from across the Internet), those from "job boards only," or those from "employer web sites only."
	You can also check the box directly below the drop-down menu to exclude leads from staffing agencies. (Some staffing agencies are known to publish "blind" ads—for jobs that don't exist—to accumulate resumes.)
	This field can also be used in combination with the previous fields.
"Salary estimate"	If you're looking for a position with a certain salary, enter the number here.
	This option can also be used in combination with the previous fields.
"Location"	Although we don't recommend limiting your work-at-home search to a geographical area (a key advantage of "virtual" work is that an employer or client can be located almost anywhere), some job seekers need or prefer to find work in certain locations, and this option enables that search.
	This feature can also be used in combination with the previous fields.
"Age—jobs published"	Use this field to set a "freshness date" for your search returns, and exclude stale leads or those you've already seen. (The drop-down menu includes a convenient setting that lets you choose to view only those leads posted since your last visit.)
	This feature can also be used in combination with the previous fields.
"Display"	The remaining options let you specify how your search results will be displayed.

Using "bad" search terms in a good way

In Chapter 5, we pointed out that the search phrase "work from home" isn't useful in most cases, because scammers so often bait their ads with it. That said, Indeed.com's search options permit us to use this "bad" search term in a good way.

Here's an example. (For Indeed's search fields not mentioned here, leave them blank.)

With the exact phrase:	Work from home
Show jobs from:	Employer web sites only
Age—Jobs published:	Within 7 days

When you've set these parameters, click on the "Find Jobs" button, and you'll get a list of all leads containing the phrase "work from home" posted on employer Websites in the past seven days.

What does this mean? By using the "employer web sites only" option, the otherwise tainted search phrase "work from home" has become more useful. Now, it's directed toward telework-related ads appearing on the Websites of actual employers, which decreases the likelihood of scams. It also excludes ads posted by individuals to job boards and other Websites, which in general are more likely to be bogus.

Even so, bear in mind that, although restricting searches to employer sites does help thin out the scams, *it's not a guarantee that all results will be trustworthy*. Many scammers are highly sophisticated, and we've seem them go to great lengths to set up "corporate" Websites that, on first glance, looked impeccably legitimate. (Much of the content is simply stolen from genuine corporate sites.)

Unfortunately, the bogus ads from these sham "employer" Websites may also end up on Indeed and other sites.

In the same vein, unscrupulous job-board hosts will sometimes register with Indeed.com as "employers," causing their often-questionable leads to show up among "employer" jobs.

Back in Chapter 4, we shared some tried-and-true tips for recognizing scams. As you implement the search strategies we detail here, remember to keep your "BS Radar" turned on and tuned in.

And "good" search terms in a better way

If the Indeed.com advanced search options work well with a "bad" search term such as "work from home," imagine what they can do with good search terms. And it's easy to get the results.

For example, just use the same fields as in the previous search. Simply change the search phrase, as we do here, to one that's more likely to yield legitimate leads and less likely to pull in scams. (For more "good search terms" like this one, see Chapter 5.)

With the exact phrase: This is a work from home position

Show jobs from: Employer web sites only

Age—Jobs published: Within 7 days

We and our Rat Race Rebellion researchers get excellent results—and you can, too—by combining advanced search options with smart search terms. Weeding out the leads from non-employer sites, and using search terms most likely to appear in job ads written by HR professionals, you can dramatically reduce the number of scams you'll have to sort through, and focus your attention instead on the most promising leads.

Getting e-mail alerts from Indeed

As with some other aggregator sites, Indeed has an "email updates" option that can make your job hunt even easier. If you find a search term that works well for you, use this feature to have Indeed search new leads automatically, and send the jobs you want directly to your inbox.

Setting up the alerts is easy. At the bottom of your search results page, you'll see a shaded box with language prompting you to sign up for "e-mail updates." Just enter your e-mail address and click the "Save Alert" button.

You'll receive an e-mail from Indeed shortly afterward. Just follow the instructions. Currently, you can opt for either daily or weekly alerts.

You may add as many search terms to your alerts list as you like. Once you've set up alerts, changing delivery frequency, altering terms, and so forth, is also easy to do.

Also worth noting, registering for an account at Indeed.com (no charge) lets users save job leads and access them from any computer.

Finding home-based jobs on SimplyHired.com

Like Indeed, SimplyHired.com—which, according to the Website, has been praised as "one of the '50 Coolest Websites' by *Time Magazine* and declared 'Best of the Web' by *BusinessWeek*"—is a job aggregator with lots of features to focus and simplify your hunt.

As we'll mention in more detail in Chapter 9, SimplyHired partners with social networking sites such as Facebook, MySpace, and others, which let job seekers network and share their education, work experience, skills, and so on, as well as connect with potential employers.

As a bonus, the site, which already has many safeguards against scam job postings, recently added a new "Flag this Job" feature, which enables job seekers to help each other by pointing to suspect, expired, or defective listings. The feature also allows Simply Hired personnel to investigate the flagged jobs and take appropriate action.

Searching for work-at-home jobs on SimplyHired.com

Simply Hired's home page is clean and simple, displaying just two search fields, for "keywords" and "location." Again, we suggest you use the advanced options, accessible by clicking the "Advanced Job Search" link just to the right of the "Search Jobs" button.

Simply Hired has many of Indeed.com's search features, but with extra options that let you refine your search even further. "Special filters," for example, let you focus your search on companies that have earned certain distinctions. These include:

Age 50+ Friendly Companies

Diversity-Friendly Companies

Dog-Friendly Companies

Eco-Friendly Companies

Forbes 200 Best Small Companies

Forbes 25 Fastest-Growing Tech Companies

Forbes 400 Best Big Companies

Fortune 100 Fastest-Growing Companies

Fortune 500

Fortune Best Companies to Work For

Fortune Best for Minorities

GLBT-Friendly Companies

Inc. 500

Non-Profit Companies

Socially Responsible Companies

Veteran-Friendly Companies

Working Mother 100 Best

You can also search leads by company size and revenue, and by the experience level a job might require (for example, "0–2 years"). Finally, a key filter also lets you confine your search to employer Websites, which, as with Indeed.com, we recommend generally for best results. (Be sure to couple it with well-crafted search phrases.)

All in all, it's a very comprehensive search package.

Simply Hired also has a unique feature that allows you to "Find Jobs by Category." You'll find it on their home page, just below the search boxes. (If you've conducted recent searches, restore the catagory list by clicking on "clear all," next to "Recent Search Activity.")

To try it out, click on "Customer Service," and you'll see a list of all leads that have been classified as customer service positions.

To find the work-from-home positions within a category, click on the category. On the page that follows, scroll down until you see the words "Refine by Keywords" in the left column.

The drop-down menu, which defaults to the "Search Within For" setting, also lets you instruct the search engine to ignore certain terms, look within certain companies, or look for certain job titles.

To try this feature, leave the default setting ("Search Within For") in place and enter the phrase "work from home" (in quotes, as there is no "exact phrase" option). Click on "Update Results" to search for that phrase within the customer service jobs on that list.

Try different words or phrases (for example, replace "work from home" with "telecommute," "anywhere," and so forth) to make sure you're not missing any jobs that might interest you.

Like Indeed, Simply Hired offers an "email alerts" option. What we like best about the Simply Hired alerts feature is the way you can fine-tune your searches and alerts.

For example, if you conduct the search we outlined here—choosing "Customer Service" from the category list on the home page, then "Refine by Keywords" with the phrase "work from home,"all you need do is enter your e-mail address in the e-mail alerts box at the bottom of your results page. Then, all of your search parameters will be saved and applied automatically to compile your alerts.

Time to experiment!

Voila, that's job aggregator sites in a nutshell. We encourage you to experiment with the two we've discussed here, and you may also want to try such sites as topusajobs.com, workhound.co.uk (UK), and juju.com. Be sure to keep an ear to the rail for newcomers to the aggregator arena, too, as the trend continues.

Now, let's turn our attention to the message boards and forums you can use to network your way to a great work-at-home job.

CHAPTER 9

Networking for Jobs, Allies, and Friends

Being at home without a job, and feeling isolated, too, is no one's idea of fun. Thankfully, the growing interest in home-based work has spawned many online networking and socializing spots to help you avoid that dread scenario.

Myriad message boards, discussion groups, forums, and chat rooms now cover home-based work—the topic could fill a separate book, so we'll stick to highlights here—as well as every other imaginable subject of interest to work-at-homers. And each venue offers an opportunity not only to network toward your perfect at-home job, but also to build alliances and friendships that can last for years, and make working at home the rewarding experience it ought to be.

Networking online 101: a brief refresher

If you've been out of the job-hunting scene for a while, networking online or off is essentially the art of building alliances—whether brief, long, casual, or intense. Done right, it's an ongoing activity, one that begins before you need a job and continues long after you've found one.

As with other e-interactions, online networking differs from the old-school variety because of the distance element. You may never meet (or even see) the person with whom you're trying to build some glue. Although you might chat on the phone, chances are that most of your rapport-building will be done by the written word. This means that all the physical nuances we rely on to convey warmth, empathy, understanding, and so forth (aka glue), are gone. The letters are all that's left.

The upshot? Be careful how you use them. Always sit back and reread before posting a critical message or sending an important e-mail. And never send something important when you've had a drink or two, or are under heavy emotional stress.

"Networking" may sound informal—and in many ways it is—but its goal is professional: a job for you.

The golden rule of networking still applies online

The same "golden rule" that holds for offline networking applies on-line as well: *Be the first to offer a favor, and, if someone beats you to it, always reciprocate.*

"But what can I offer if I'm out of work?" you may wonder. Not to worry—the list is long. Here are just a few helpful offers you might make a fellow networker:

◆ Critique a resume or cover letter.

◆ Role-play a telephone interview.

◆ Send links to relevant news, executive interviews, company profiles, and so on.

◆ Put him or her in touch with someone who knows or works in their field.

Don't spill the beans

As you build your contacts—and particularly in the beginning, when joblessness, rejection, or isolation may have tamped down your morale, and made you feel vulnerable—be on guard to resist the natural urge to confide everything to newfound online acquaintances.

Speaking freely and sharing sensitive personal details on the phone or in person is fine with trusted friends, but doing so casually online can be disastrous. Not only may your remarks persist for years—to be forwarded or clucked over by anyone—but potential allies may also quickly form a mistaken impression of you, and shy away from helping you.

Confiding troubles you're having at home, for example, can quickly discourage someone from recommending you to a boss who seeks teleworkers with a stable and quiet home environment—which is precisely what many employers not only want, but insist upon. Other potential allies may be wary of a person perceived (rightfully or otherwise) to be needy or clingy.

And finally, employers, too—as many younger free-posting e-dwellers have discovered to their chagrin—often peruse the Internet (including newer venues such as Twitter), doing their own "due diligence" on the people who would like to work for them.

Chatting and chumming (and networking)

Besides their value as networking sites, online communities and similar venues offer a great place to forge friendships, build mentor-mentee relationships, and develop casual but emotionally nourishing acquaintanceships.

Indeed, for many home-based workers, an online social circle can spell the difference between contentment, success, and confidence, and painful isolation, disconnectedness, and "species deprivation syndrome." (This is where you find yourself waiting politely for your goldfish to reply to your question about something you saw on *Oprah*. Even Elmo doesn't do *that*.)

Humor aside, you'll see the point when you consider how much of our social lives grow from—and depend upon—our brick-and-mortar workplaces. There among the cubes we mark and celebrate birthdays and births, christenings and *quinceañeras*, bar and bat mitzvahs, promotions, vacations, and retirements, and are invited to everything from picnics and barbeques to bowling, softball games, dates, and the altar. (Indeed, in many ways, job-sites have replaced the "bedroom communities" of the suburbs as our true places of community.)

So until the numbers of teleworkers finally reach levels where they warm up the suburbs—and the suburbs themselves give us better places to bond by day than fast-food outlets and hurry-through cafes—the Internet will continue to be the primary social umbilical cord for most home-based workers.

(Coworking centers—where teleworkers can gather face-to-face to get their social fix while they finish that memo, Microsoft PowerPoint presentation, or blog post—have popped up here and there, but it may be a while before they come to the mall near you. In the meantime, examples include Office Nomads, at officenomads.com, and Cubes & Crayons, at cubesandcrayons.com.)

So without further ado, here are some of the online gathering places we love or have heard great things about.

Work-at-home forums

These venues are geared toward people who work from home or want to, and relevant topics or themes. As a reminder, when you visit any forum or message board, job leads and related information may not have been screened, so be sure to tune up your BS (Big Scam) radar—which should be in good working order when you look at any job lead online—before moving ahead.

WorkPlaceLikeHome.com— our favorite work-at-home forum

WorkPlaceLikeHome (or WPLH, as it's known in work-at-home circles) is our top choice among the gathering places, and we always recommend it in our virtual-career training programs. The reasons are many, but the one that stands out is *the people*—its members. (Just for the record, we have no stake in this or any third-party forum or message board.)

Somehow, the folks behind WPLH have managed to pull together a group of more than 40,000 individuals who get along unusually well—sharing job leads and answers, hirer feedback, interview tips, employee insights, friendship, laughter, sympathy, and more—just as they might in a close-knit, cul-de-sac community.

If you're new to working at home, we have another reason for recommending WPLH. If you've frequented online message boards, you've probably encountered the occasional prima donna (or don) wearing a "knowledge tiara," and doling out information with an air of peevishness and contempt for the people who inconvenience her or him with a "stupid" question. Such "boaster posters" are remarkably absent from WPLH—despite the presence of many long-term participants, with extensive knowledge to share. Accordingly, "newbies" can ask questions without fear of being snubbed for not knowing the "basics."

The forum includes boards for work and non-work topics, and moderators who moderate rather than police. Even so, they move swiftly to correct and, if necessary, evict misbehaving posters (that is, those intentionally starting arguments, making personal attacks, posting scams, and so on).

Drilling down, you'll find a general "work-at-home jobs" board, as well as dozens devoted to specific companies and industries. On the non-work side are boards for "random babble," and others focusing on themes such as surviving the economy, family and children, reading, entertainment, humor, and so forth.

WPLH Member Feedback

No forum is perfect, of course—we all have unique personalities and preferences, and it would be an odd place indeed where everyone fit in— but WPLH's members seem to like their hangout. Here is a typical (unedited) comment from a member who wrote us about the site:

> *Visiting this site on a daily basis (multiple times a day) keeps me inspired and gives me hope that I can help pay off our debt, put away some savings for our children, and do it all from home, without daycare expenses and fixed schedules. I know this can be done because I read the success stories every day, and since I joined this site, I have added thousands of dollars to our family budget (most of this paid some bills, but some went to having some fun, paying cash for it, too).*
> —WPLH member since 2007

WAHM.com

Owned by Internet Brands, Inc., WAHM.com (the acronym stands for "work-at-home moms") describes itself as an "online magazine," and boasts more than 80,000 members. (Men are welcome, too.) The site houses robust forums with message boards for telecommuting, direct marketing, religion, advice, business topics, and more.

We visit WAHM.com periodically, and throught the years have found the posts on its "telecommuting moms" board especially informative. Many members have been with the site for years, too, bringing a wealth of knowledge to those just starting out in the work-at-home arena.

WhyDoWork.com

We remember when this Canada-based site was launched in 2004. Toni Kistner, a writer then with *Network World*, wrote to ask if we knew anything about it. Because we didn't, we looked, and have been tracking them ever since. They've grown into a useful resource for aspiring work-at-homers.

WhyDoWork.com focuses on work-at-home jobs and businesses. With more than 40,000 members, their message boards are fairly active. (Bear in mind, such things wax and wane, so you may find more or less activity when you visit.)

Though not as eclectic as the two previous sites, WhyDoWork.com does a good job of covering the basics, with boards for work-at-home jobs and employers, and support for stay-at-home moms and dads. There's a board dedicated to "Get Paid To" projects and gigs, too.

Other boards include affiliate marketing, investment programs, and similar opportunities of interest to many in the work-at-home arena.

FreelanceMom.com

This site has about 12,000 members and a great reputation. Click on the "work at home forum" link to reach the boards, where discussions include finding jobs, starting businesses, venting, raising children, recipes—the gamut.

Broader sites with work-at-home message boards

Certain broad groups and larger professional categories such as moms, writers, military spouses, retirees, and so on, have many members interested in working at home. Consequently, sites or communities that were developed to serve those groups will also often include message boards related to home-based or "virtual" work.

Here's a sampling:

CafeMom.com

Focus: mothers

CafeMom is the largest social networking site for mothers, with message boards on myriad topics. To get to the boards (or "groups"), click on the "groups" tab and select the "find groups" option. Here, you can enter keywords to find a group that interests you, or click on the "view the full list of groups by category" link.

For boards pertaining to work/employment, click on the "work and money" category and you'll find thousands of groups. Below the list you'll see links to help you refine your search. Try clicking on "work at home" and "work from home" to access discussions on those topics.

iVillage.com

Focus: women

iVillage, owned by media company NBC Universal, was the first major site established exclusively for women. As with CafeMom, there are message boards on every topic imaginable.

Click on the "message boards" link at the top of the page, then either scan the boards listed, or use the search feature to find "work at home" and "work from home" boards.

Military.com

Focus: U.S. military and family members

Military.com, with 10 million members (we're columnists there, covering virtual and home-based careers), is the largest U.S. military membership organization. It's owned by Monster Worldwide (Monster.com).

To navigate, click on the "community" link and select "discussion boards," where you'll find many dialogues involving careers and employment, including work from home.

Eons.com

Focus: Baby Boomers (retirees and pre-retirees)

Eons, a social networking site primarily for Boomers, was founded by Jeff Taylor, who also founded Monster.com. The site has a number of message boards for current and aspiring work-at-homers.

To reach the boards, mouse over the "groups" tab at the top of the page, then click on "browse by category." Explore the various "money & careers" boards, or use the search function with terms such as "work at home" and "work from home."

AbsoluteWrite.com

Focus: writers

This site is for freelance writers of every kind: playwrights, screenwriters, novelists, poets, bloggers, comic book writers, and others. (Freelance writers often work from home.) If you write, or aspire to, it's a great resource.

With more than 17,000 members, the forums are bursting at the seams with information and advice. Topics include self-promotion, technical help, blogging, novels, self-publishing, paying markets, and more.

VANetworking.com
(Virtual Assistant Networking Forum)

Focus: Virtual Assistants

Here, bear with us for a moment as we get sentimental; the virtual assistant (VA) industry is dear to our hearts. Chris is credited with having founded the industry in 1995 (when she launched the first VA practice, MyStaff, from her basement in rural Connecticut), and our first book—*The 2-Second Commute: Join the Exploding Ranks of Freelance Virtual Assistants*—focuses on how to grow a VA business. We also designed and deliver VA training programs for the U.S. Air Force, Army, and so forth, and deliver similar training to the U.S. Department of State.

But back to brass tacks. The Virtual Assistant Networking Forum (VANetworking.com) has a very active international membership that discusses all facets of launching, running, and marketing a VA business. (VAs typically work from home.) To reach the forums, click on the "enter members area" link.

Job-search sites with message boards

Many of the major job-search sites, realizing the importance of discussions and community-building in the job-hunting and career-development field, have added forums. Although they may not be as well organized—yet—as those on sites that specialize in forums, the conversations can definitely be worthwhile.

Indeed.com

As noted in the previous chapter, Indeed.com is a job-search aggregator site that draws its leads from thousands of sources across the Internet.

You can reach their forums by clicking on the "forums" link at the bottom of the home page. The forums are broken down into basic topics: company (discussions regarding specific companies), job (covering particular jobs or job types), city (converse with job seekers and employers in given geographical areas), and general (dialogues regarding interviewing, success stories, resume tips, and so forth).

Monster.com

To access forums at Monster.com, click on the "community" link at the bottom of the home page. Forums are divided into five categories: Get the Job, On the Job, Industry Insights, Stimulus Jobs, and Hot Topics. Each category has numerous sub-categories.

One path to meet new people is the "Hot Topics" section, where you'll find the "Break Room." Want to blow off some steam? (Always a healthy thing in the job-search process.) Check out the "Vent!" forum.

Larger social networking sites and "virtual worlds"

There are times when the Internet seems to consist of two Websites: YouTube and Facebook. And when these get boring, you can don an avatar in a virtual world, such as Second Life, and talk to other avatars about everything under the code-generated sun. You can even make actual money in virtual real estate, or selling virtual goods such as avatar designs—from home.

Facebook alone has generated numerous books—as has Second Life—and they're changing almost by the minute, so we'll only touch on these sites here. For more, stop by Amazon, Barnes & Noble, or your local library, or, if you haven't already, dip a toe at the sites themselves.

Social networking explodes

Sites like MySpace and Facebook were unknown a few years ago, but have since surged across the Internet. Now, it's safe to say that Facebook, at least—the current leader among social networking sites—is becoming a significant destination for work-at-homers, along with everyone else.

The list of social networking sites is growing, too. (Though where the sector will be a few years from now is anyone's guess.) In addition to the mega-sites, there are LinkedIn, Spoke, hi5, Bebo, Orkut, PerfSpot, and many more.

Even job-aggregator sites such as SimplyHired (see Chapter 8) are jumping into the social-networking mix, and their enthusiasm for Facebook is clear. When we spoke with them recently, they had this to say:

SimplyHired leverages the power of Facebook and other major social networks (such as MySpace, LinkedIn, Plaxo, etc.) which enable friends to share their education, work experience and skills with each other. For example, many job seekers connect with possible employers via Facebook's "Workin' It" application and "I Am [Profession]" tools. With more than 28,558 monthly active users, "I Am Nurse" is one of the most popular Facebook applications, allowing nurses to network and share what it means to be a nurse with friends.

Facebook is free and easy to join. If you decide to add your name to the throng, look us up at Rat Race Rebellion and say hi.

Avatar friends and customers

Virtual worlds such as Second Life and There have figured prominently in the media, and with younger generations hanging out online in Webkinz World, MapleStory, and myriad "gamer" worlds, the trend may stick.

In the meantime, you can make friends, network, and meet employers, too, on Second Life. (A number of telework-friendly companies, including Sun and IBM, have a presence there.)

Some "SL" members are also making money in-world (often from home) buying and renting real estate, custom-designing avatars, and working in SL stores and other establishments. (Caution: As in real life, not all roles and businesses are "PG"-rated.) You can also work from home for Linden Lab itself, SL's owner, in customer relations, software coding, and more. (For details, see lindenlab.com.)

FYOF: find your own forum

As we've noted, the forums and other venues we've featured here are just the tip of the online iceberg, and you'll want to explore others, too. Thankfully, finding forums that suit your unique needs, personality type, and line of work is not that different from finding jobs using the right search terms.

For example, if you're a graphic artist who would like to commune online with others in your field, try Googling with searches such as:

◆ "message board" + "graphic artists"
◆ "chat room" + "graphic artists"
◆ "forum for graphic artists"

But regardless of your niche or situation, you may be pleasantly surprised by how many of your peers are already networking and getting to know one another online, and how easy it is to join them.

CHAPTER 10

Virtual and Telework-Friendly Companies

Since the 1990s, when the Internet began to spark the growth of distributed work, an increasing number of companies have either "gone virtual" (often with a core managerial team remaining in a company office), or adopted programs to allow employees to work offsite, usually one or more days per week.

In fact, according to *Fortune*'s 2009 list of "100 Best Companies to Work For," 84 allow employees to telecommute at least 20 percent of the time. Contrast this with *Fortune*'s 1999 "100 Best" list, when only 18 companies allowed telecommuting. This remarkable 366-percent increase is just one indication of the growing acceptance of distributed workers.

Companies use a variety of terms to label their telework programs: e-working, flexible work, remote work, mobility programs, distributed work, ROWE (Results-Only Work Environment), and others. Regardless of the moniker, the programs all involve employees working somewhere besides "company HQ."

Because the focus of this book is pragmatic—to help you find a work-at-home job—we'll skip the typical statistics-heavy analysis of why companies adopt telework programs. But a glance at how employers benefit from telework can only help make your job hunt more effective, so we've summarized some of the key advantages here:

205

Recruiting and Retention

◆ The ability to draw the best workers from a global talent pool.

◆ Telework is fast becoming a talent magnet, giving companies with a remote-work program a competitive edge in recruiting.

◆ Increased employee satisfaction = increased employee retention.

◆ Facilitates hiring and retention of people with disabilities and workers who relocate on a regular basis (for example, "trailing spouses").

Reduced Costs

◆ Lower real estate and other "brick-and-mortar" costs.

◆ Reduction in health insurance costs due to decreased commuting-related illnesses (stress-related disease, obesity, and so forth).

◆ Lower absenteeism and tardiness.

Increased Productivity

◆ Expansion of company service hours (multiple time zones, shifts, and so forth).

◆ Lower absenteeism and tardiness.

◆ Fewer "walk-in" work interruptions.

◆ Enhanced performance as telecommuters work (rather than commute) during their most productive hours.

◆ Greater business continuity during disruptions due to natural disaster, severe weather, power outage, mass illness, transit strikes, and other unforeseen events.

Further, companies with telework programs increasingly reap valuable public relations, media, and recruiting advantages in being seen as "family-friendly," "pro–work/life balance," "green," and so forth. And with growing legislative and treaty initiatives to combat global warming, companies may soon enjoy significant tax and related financial benefits as well.

National companies with telework arrangements

Following is a selection of companies and organizations (a number of which you'll also find mentioned in Chapter 6) that have implemented telework programs, or maintain to some degree a virtual workforce.

To get an inside look at hiring needs, applications vs. openings, and other factors, we interviewed a number of companies. As you'll see, these are primarily in the field of home-based customer service (aka "homeshoring"), which not only continues to expand, but has also sparked much job-seeker interest. These firms are indicated in **bold**. (The interviews themselves follow.) If a listed company's workforce is predominantly home-based, the firm is marked with an asterisk (*).

For more detail on a given company and to check for current openings, see the company's Website. Just search with the company name—use quotes for multiple words—on Google, Bing, and so on. (Please note that, since recruiting needs fluctuate, companies listed here may or may not have positions open. If not, bookmark the site and check back regularly, as positions often appear without notice and can fill quickly.)

Accenture	Adobe Systems
Aetna	Aflac
Alcon Laboratories	**Alpine Access***
Allergan	Allstate Insurance Company
American Airlines	American Express
Apple Computer	**Arise Virtual Solutions***
Bank of America	Bechtel Corporation
Best Buy	Blue Cross/Blue Shield
Boeing Company	Booz Allen Hamilton
Boston Consulting Group	Capella University*
Chevron	Cigna
Cisco Systems	Citibank
Colgate Palmolive	Compaq
Dell Computer	Deloitte
Dupont	Eastman Kodak Company
Equitable Life Assurance	Ericsson Inc.

Ernst & Young

eBay

Fannie Mae

Federal Express

Fujitsu

Gannett

Geico

Girl Scouts of America

Google

Herman Miller

Hewlett-Packard

Hitachi America

Holiday Inn Worldwide

HomeBanc Mortgage

H&R Block

IBM

Intel

Intuit

John Hancock Insurance

Kaiser Permanente

KellyConnect®*

KPMG

LiveOps*

Lockheed Martin

Manpower

Marriott

McGraw Hill

Microsoft

MITRE

Motorola

Mutual of Omaha

NEW

Nike

Nortel Networks

Oracle

Proctor & Gamble

Raytheon Systems

Shell Oil Company

Sprint

Sun Microsystems

Symantec

Team Double-Click®*

Texas Instruments

VIPdesk*

Xerox

Interviews with selected companies

Interviews are given in alphabetical order by company name. Where companies provide hiring estimates or projections, please bear in mind that these are "best guesses." As mentioned, workforce needs fluctuate, and are also notoriously hard to predict, so be sure to check the company's Website for current openings.

Alpine Access (alpineaccess.com)

Part of the growing "homeshoring" movement (home-based call center agents), Alpine Access hires at-home Customer Care Professionals (CCPs) across the United States. To learn more, we chatted via e-mail with Remi Killeen-Weber, the company's recruitment manager.

Authors: What are the three most important credentials for a CCP applicant to possess?

Remi Killeen-Weber:

1. Proven ability to successfully work from their home office.
   a. Ability to work independently.
   b. Strong work ethic.
   c. Self-reliant and self-motivated.
2. Excellent listening and problem-solving skills, while establishing professional and trustworthy rapport with the customer.
3. Have high to expert computer navigational/data entry skills Required to be an "internet athlete."

Authors: What are the red flags that most often disqualify applicants from becoming a CCP?

Remi Killeen-Weber:

1. Poor work ethic.
2. Demonstrated pattern of not fulfilling commitments.
3. Not able to work independently, problem-solve, and not self-motivated.

Authors: Approximately how many CCPs does Alpine Access expect to hire in 2010?

Remi Killeen-Weber: 3,000

Authors: How many applications, on average, does Alpine Access receive per month for CCP positions?

Remi Killeen-Weber: 5,000

Authors: What promotional opportunities exist (if any) for exceptional CCPs?

Remi Killeen-Weber: CCPs have opportunities to be promoted to coach, team lead, and management positions within the company.

Arise Virtual Solutions (arise.com)

Similar to Alpine Access, Arise, a pioneer of the homeshoring movement, utilizes at-home agents. Unlike Alpine Access, however, which hires home-based agents as employees, Arise contracts with its home-based agents as independent contractors. Agents, known as "Arise Certified Professionals," must also form a limited liability company (LLC) or similar legal entity before contracting with Arise for work.

(There are pros and cons to each status [employee and freelancer]. For example, employees may earn less, but sometimes receive benefits and paid training. Freelancers may earn more, but receive no benefits, and must sometimes pay for their training. As with other companies, homeshoring firms differ as to which status their agents will have. For details, see our list of 85+ hirers of home-based agents at *www.ratracerebellion.com/CS_Comparison.html*. For IRS guidance, see IRS.gov, and search "independent contractor vs. employee," with quotes.)

To learn more about Arise and its agents, we chatted via e-mail with Jared Fletcher, vice president, Strategic Sourcing and VSC Operations.

Authors: Apart from the legal-entity requirements, what are the three most important credentials for an applicant to possess?

Jared Fletcher: Because Arise Certified Professionals are independent business owners, who enter into business-to-business relationships with Arise Virtual Solutions, Inc. and select the clients for which they provide service, the three most important groupings of credentials for them to possess are: 1) An entrepreneurial spirit, including self-motivation that enables them to work successfully virtually, and passion for our clients' brands; 2) strong customer contact skills and expertise; and 3) the correct tools: an organized, quiet work environment and the required technology.

Authors: What are the red flags that most often disqualify applicants from becoming Arise Certified Professionals?

Jared Fletcher: Some red flags that indicate applicants would not be ideal matches to Arise's model include: 1) a failed background check, 2) demonstration of unprofessional written and spoken communications, and 3) indications that he or she lacks self-motivation.

Authors: Approximately how many Certified Professionals does the company expect to hire in 2010?

Jared Fletcher: Arise does not "hire" agents; instead, we certify and enter into B2B relationships with qualified agents. In 2010, we expect to certify and contract with thousands of Arise Certified Professionals.

Authors: How many applications, on average, does Arise receive per month?

Jared Fletcher: On average, Arise receives 7,000 completed profiles per month.

Authors: What promotional opportunities exist (if any) for exceptional Arise Certified Professionals?

Jared Fletcher: Because Arise Certified Professionals are their own employers, their opportunities and potential to grow their businesses is in their hands. As part of the B2B relationship, Arise rewards performance, including increases in compensation for exceeding predetermined client expectations. Additionally, Arise offers a few supervisory and instructor positions for which qualified Arise Certified Professionals can apply.

KellyConnect® (Kelly Services, Inc.; kellyconnect.com)

In the past few years, staffing giant Kelly has moved into the customer-contact arena as well, with "KellyConnect." As they explain on their site, "The KellyConnect program provides full service staffing and management solutions for a variety of contact center environments including customer service, sales, market research, collections, and help desks."

To learn more, we spoke with Jonathan Means, senior vice president and general manager, who oversees the KellyConnect program.

Authors: What are the top skills and traits that Kelly looks for in candidates for home-based customer-service positions?

Jonathan Means: We look for general skills and specific traits, depending on the type of work the agent will be doing (for example, customer service, help desk, collections, etc.). In general, we're looking for customer-service skills, good listening skills, the ability to multitask, and a strong likelihood to remain on the job. Our testing process, of course, helps us determine if candidates will be effective.

Authors: What is the most common disqualifier for applicants for Kelly's home-based customer-service positions?

Jonathan Means: The home office environment needs to be professional. Applicants should recognize this isn't a substitute for childcare. There should be no background noise. Our goal is to offer our clients' customers an experience that is in fact better than the "brick-and-mortar" customer-contact experience.

Authors: Looking into the near future, what changes (if any) do you see in Kelly's home-based job offerings?

Jonathan Means: We see a number of directions that KellyConnect can and will go in. Nursing triage is an area we're interested in. Legal processing, with the potential involvement of lawyers and paralegals, is something we're interested in as well.

LiveOps (liveops.com)

An innovative Silicon Valley–based company, LiveOps also offers outsourced customer-contact support, with more than 20,000 home-based agents across North America.

Similar to Arise, VIPdesk, and others, LiveOps engages agents as independent contractors rather than employees. Agent categories include inbound sales-related services (handling calls from infomercials, for example), processing delivery and carry-out orders for casual-dining vendors (pizza, for example), handling bilingual Spanish-English and French-English inbound commercial calls, and so forth. LiveOps also engages home-based independent insurance agents to handle inbound calls from prospective insurance customers.

As mentioned in Chapter 11, LiveOps also recently launched LiveWork (livework.com), a marketplace where freelancers can team up and take on larger business process outsourcing (BPO) contracts.

To learn more about LiveOps' agent work, we chatted via e-mail with Tim Whipple, VP of LiveOps Virtual Contact Center.

Authors: What are the most important credentials for a LiveOps Independent Agent applicant to possess?

Tim Whipple: The majority of contract work offered by LiveOps Virtual Call Center is teleservices, and therefore it is important for individuals to have qualities such as the following:

- ◆ Self-motivated—They are freelancers and therefore must be motivated and enthusiastic about operating their own business.

- ◆ Reading ability—They must be able to read a script with enthusiasm as well as proper articulation, tone, pace—without sounding like they are reading a script.

- ◆ Sales skills—The ability to turn inquiries into sales using positive persuasion, persistence rebuttals, and product knowledge.

◆ Strong vocal communications skills, which includes empathy skills to express interest and understanding via phone.

Authors: What are the red flags that most often disqualify applicants from becoming a LiveOps Independent Agent?

Tim Whipple:

◆ Poor voice quality.

◆ Inability to pass basic certification.

◆ Lack of technical skill to set up and operate a personal computer.

◆ Reliability when committing to scheduling and taking the appropriate certification courses. (This requires such skills as self-discipline and self-motivation, because they are independent contractors and therefore are in the driver's seat when it comes to building their business.)

◆ Unwillingness, inability, or unsuited to sell products over the phone (as opposed to simply taking an order).

Authors: As a rough estimate, how many agents would LiveOps project to hire in 2010?

Tim Whipple: Liveops does not hire agents but rather the agents are "freelancers" and contract their services to Liveops customers. There are a number of variables that need to be considered in this prediction, including the fact that "freelance agents" opt in to work, and it also depends on business demand by our customers for contracted services. In 2009, the company saw demand from its customers for individuals with bilingual skills—especially Spanish—as well as individuals who were licensed insurance agents.

If we examine the past few years of growth, we would estimate that the freelance agent community may increase by 2,000.

Authors: How many applications, on average, does LiveOps receive per month for agent positions?

Tim Whipple: About 14,000 people start the application process each month and about 3,000 will complete the application process each month. In general, through the application process, we invite approximately 2 percent of the total applicants per month to contract services to LiveOps.

Authors: What promotional opportunities exist (if any) for exceptional agents (for example, to supervisory positions)?

Tim Whipple: LiveOps is revolutionizing the world of work with its independent agent model. It is not about promotions but opportunities—just as one would consider getting more opportunities out of a partnership relationship. That is what these independent agents have with LiveOps.

Also, our performance-based model presents opportunities for high-performing independent agents to get preference in scheduling and business opportunities that come along. Also, top-performing independent agents have the opportunity to make as much as twice what a call center agent in a traditional brick-and-mortar center would make.

N.E.W. Customer Service Companies, Inc. (newcorp.com)

Founded in 1983, *NEW* operates 10 U.S.–based call centers and has approximately 1,300 home-based Customer Care Representatives (CCRs), with more than 5,800 employees overall.

Similar to Jet Blue and some other firms, *NEW* requires its agents to complete face-to-face training before working at home. Training is offered in 12 locations in various states, and, as the company mentions in the interview that follows, it expects to increase those locations in the coming year, and has not ruled out an online training program down the road.

For more detail, we chatted via e-mail with Donna Neale, *NEW* vice president, Contact Center Operations.

Authors: What are the three most important credentials for a CCR applicant to possess?

Donna Neale: In the *NEW* contact center environment—both our virtual work-at-home program and our brick-and-mortar centers—two core skill sets come to mind which are equally critical for a CCR applicant to possess. At *NEW*, we deliver a high degree of customer care using state-of-the-art technology, so it's very important that our Customer Care Representatives possess a *solid technical aptitude* to navigate the various applications we use to track, document, and enhance our customer experience. It's also equally important for CCRs to have a *strong phone presence*. Due to the nature of the job, it's imperative that the CCR can clearly articulate to ensure the customer receives a positive experience.

Confidence and *self-discipline* go hand-in-hand, particularly in the work-at-home environment, as another key characteristic of a good CCR applicant. Confidence is necessary to interact with both pleased and disgruntled customers and to be able to reach that initial hurdle when that CCR embarks on that call which can be unpredictable and challenging with every new customer interaction. And self-discipline becomes vital to home CCRs to keep themselves continuously motivated and focused on their work.

In addition to these skill sets and characteristics, it is also imperative that the applicant possess at least a *high school diploma* or *GED. Previous customer care experience* is preferred and will be factored into advancement opportunities.

Authors: As a rough estimate, how many virtual CCRs do you expect to hire in 2010?

Donna Neale: *NEW* plans to hire approximately 1,200 CCRs for its virtual contact centers in 2010.

Authors: What's the one sure way to get fired from a CCR position?

Donna Neale: *NEW* does not tolerate any violations of company policies including mistreatment of customers, poor performance or attendance.

Authors: What plans does *NEW* have to increase the state distribution of its training sites, and/or shift to an online training model?

Donna Neale: *NEW* is continually researching and evaluating opportunities to expand its programs and ways to advance its operations using technology. While new locations have not been identified at this time, *NEW* does plan to grow its training sites across the United States through 2010. Due to the extensive nature of *NEW*'s business, 4 to 6 week face-to-face trainings are conducted to ensure the new CCRs are comfortable with the program, learn the corporate culture and core values of *NEW*, and can fully navigate the computer applications. While in-person training best conveys the quality customer care *NEW* strives for today, we have not fully ruled out some type of online training program down the road if it could achieve similar results as we see with our site-based trainings.

Sun Microsystems (sun.com)

Now 14 years old (per Sun's Website), Sun's award-winning OpenWork program has long been a leader in the telework movement. In addition to significant environmental benefits, the "work-from-anywhere" program has improved job satisfaction and enabled Sun to save millions of dollars in real estate costs.

For more, we chatted via e-mail with Kristi McGee, senior director, OpenWork Services Group, who referred our query to Heidi Pate, senior product marketing manager, OpenWork Services Group.

Authors: What are the employee eligibility criteria for Sun's OpenWork program? Does Sun look for certain skills or traits in a candidate?

Heidi Pate: Every employee is eligible to participate in the OpenWork program. We have a category selection process that provides employees with the opportunity to carefully consider his or her work arrangement in light of job needs, workgroup's needs, and personal circumstances and preferences.

The ability of an employee to participate in their desired category is at the discretion of management. In making these decisions and in considering the impact on business and workgroup needs, managers give strong consideration to the employees' preferred category. Generally, these needs should not be in conflict if the employee and manager have been objective in their assessment.

Authors: Given the cohesion issues inherent in distributed workforces, what tips or pointers could you share with teleworkers generally for assuring that things run smoothly with the home office and fellow team members?

Heidi Pate: Advances in technology are rapidly increasing the opportunities that knowledge workers have to work across the network. To stay engaged and work effectively with coworkers in a distributed work environment, it's vital to stay connected through communication tools that leverage voice, data, video, instant messaging (IM), shared calendars, and online professional and personal profiles.

Create opportunities to develop a rich variety of interactions to pull teams and communities together. To easily communicate and share as a team, each contributor needs to become proficient with relevant tools and technologies and be visible to and accessible by others over the network. Team members need to take advantage of available technologies and methods of working over the network to better communicate, gain access to, and share ideas, information, and knowledge with remote coworkers. When teams are not collocated, spontaneous and informal communications—such as instant messaging (IM), chat room, or a threaded Wiki discussion—are just as important to feel connected as a team as planned meetings.

In order to learn about OpenWork, prepare themselves for change, and to quickly become effective in the new work environment, Sun has established Web-based and classroom OpenWork training courses for both employees and managers, whose needs differ. Focal areas include time management and personal organization, remote management, staying connected to coworkers, and distance collaboration. Another important area of OpenWork education and training involves providing managers with the skills, tools, and support required to excel at remote management.

Authors: In your opinion, what are the three worst mistakes a teleworker can make?

Heidi Pate: To stay connected and feel part of a multi-dimensional community, employees need to make the commitment to be visible, reachable, and online—and to embrace network options for connecting and cultivating ways to engage with each other.

Three mistakes would be to fail to:

1. Embrace and utilize technologies that make it possible to connect, engage, communicate, and share with your manager and coworkers.
2. Be visible to your manager and coworkers (online status and availability on the network via presence indicators such as instant messaging, shared online calendars).
3. Fulfill commitments that you've made with your manager and coworkers; not deliver work at agreed-upon time and level of quality.

Authors: What are the plans for the OpenWork program going out the next few years? For example, are participant numbers expected to grow, contract, or remain the same? Are parameters or guidelines expected to change?

Heidi Pate: OpenWork participation is expected to continue to grow and trend upward. Work patterns are changing, and at the end of March 2009, almost 18,200 employees were working away from the office one or two days a week. A recent Sun study indicated about 70 percent of our workforce engages in mobile work, requiring most employees to collaborate remotely during the work week.

When employees do come to a Sun office, they mainly want to collaborate with coworkers rather than focus on "heads-down" work. This shift to a more mobile worker is now the norm and not the exception at Sun. Our next generation work environments are open, collaborative, and interactive with design based on communities and neighborhoods—reconfigurable design with less "built" and more eco-friendly environments.

We are focused on providing robust distance collaboration technologies including high-definition video conferencing and tools for application and desktop sharing, along with expanded follow-me telephony and wireless Internet access across all Sun sites. Increased support for managing distributed teams and new hire assimilation, social networking available at an enterprise level, and ongoing development of learning courses on collaboration to build skills when working with virtual teams are also ongoing priorities.

Team Double-Click (teamdoubleclick.com)

Based in Colorado, Team Double-Click is a virtual staffing agency that provides virtual office assistants and virtual real estate assistants to home-based and other small businesses.

For the inside viewpoint, we chatted via e-mail with Gayle Buske, co-founder, president, and CEO.

Authors: What are the three most important credentials for a Team Double-Click virtual assistant (VA) applicant to possess?

Gayle Buske: (1) Great communication, (2) technical skills (Internet savvy), and (3) self-discipline.

Authors: What are the three worst mistakes that you see VAs make?

Gayle Buske: (1) Showing up late for interviews, (2) rudeness during the interview, and (3) not being well-trained in virtual skills.

Authors: On average, approximately how many applications for VA work do you receive per month?

Gayle Buske: About 800.

Authors: Pulling out the crystal ball, for what types of work do you expect to see your greatest need for VAs in the near future?

Gayle Buske: Honestly, for all areas of virtual assisting. With the shifting economy, businesses are slimming back on in-office staff and looking to virtual assistants for help. We firmly believe that this economy will create a semi-permanent mindset shift in business owners and a more thrifty business owner. This plays to the benefits virtual assistants offer. We believe that the virtual assistant industry will continue to grow exponentially over the next several years and beyond.

VIPdesk (vipdesk.com)

Launched in 1997, Virginia-based VIPdesk provides high-end customer-care services to more than 70 blue-chip clients, with hundreds of home-based representatives across the United States and Canada.

The company utilizes both home-based concierges and call center representatives, and refers to the latter as "Brand Ambassadors." (In the interview that follows, for simplicity's sake the two categories have been grouped under the term "Home-Based Customer Care Representative.")

To learn more, we chatted via e-mail with Mary Naylor, CEO and cofounder of VIPdesk.

Authors: What are the three most important credentials for a VIPdesk Home-Based Customer Care Representative to possess?

Mary Naylor: The first thing that we look for in a Home-Based Customer Care Representative is superb customer service skills. We look for candidates who desire to serve, are customer focused, have an excellent tone of service, are resourceful and able to troubleshoot challenges.

The second sought-after quality is self-motivation, which is essential for working in the virtual environment. Since you do not have anyone looking over your shoulder while working, it is important to motivate yourself and do what is asked of you to the best of your ability.

The third quality is strong multitasking skills. Home-Based Customer Care Representatives use multiple systems—constantly clicking from one application to another, from a phone call to an online application—and must be able to do so with ease and without distraction.

Authors: What are the red flags that most often disqualify applicants from becoming a VIPdesk Home-Based Customer Care Representative?

Mary Naylor: When screening candidates, we approach the process by taking into consideration the "full picture." This means, we consider every detail during the recruiting process—from the promptness of responding to e-mails, the professionalism of communications, enthusiasm, work history, resume and cover letter, to knowledge of our company and clients. We believe things that happen during the qualification process will be replicated while interacting with our clients.

In addition, we frown upon lack of professionalism in vocal and written communication, and a lack of follow-up. Home-Based Customer Care Representatives will be sending e-mails on behalf of our clients, so we expect them to use proper grammar, spelling, punctuation, and sentence structure. We really do read every written item sent to us!

We also look closely at responsiveness on the part of the Customer Care Representative. We assume that if someone doesn't follow up with us in the qualification process, more than likely, there won't be follow-up with customers. Timely responses, taking the initiative, and following up on something you say you will do does matter!

Along the same lines, we also find a poor tone in calls with our recruiters to be a deal-breaker. We expect that the way you are going to represent yourself with VIPdesk is how you are going to carry yourself when representing clients.

Finally, lack of availability is definitely a problem. We aren't just offering "guidelines" when we provide program hour requirements—we expect that candidates will be able to meet those expectations.

Authors: Approximately how many Home-Based Customer Care Representatives does VIPdesk expect to hire in 2010?

Mary Naylor: We are expecting to work with several hundred (possibly even as many as a thousand!) new Home-Based Customer Care Representatives in 2010. Our current clients are increasing the amount of work that we do together, and we are constantly expanding our business with new clients and new industries. Further, due to the seasonal nature of some of our retail clients, we are always recruiting seasonal Customer Care Representatives in the late summer and fall to handle the holiday rush.

Authors: How many applications, on average, does VIPdesk receive per month?

Mary Naylor: We receive thousands of applications per month. Something to note is that VIPdesk strives to provide the highest level of service and quality to its clients, and therefore, only candidates who match our values and show it during the qualification process are successful.

Authors: What promotional opportunities exist for exceptional Home-Based Customer Care Representatives?

Mary Naylor: VIPdesk strongly believes in promoting from within. There are many former Home-Based Customer Care Representatives who have taken corporate jobs.

—•═◆═•—

Now that you've had a closer look at virtual and telework-oriented companies, we'll show you how to find freelance projects online and work from home "gig-to-gig."

CHAPTER 11

Freelancing at Home Gig-to-Gig

Web designers, proofreaders, writers, artists, translators, and many other professionals often work project-by-project—or "gig-to-gig"—in a freelance or independent-contractor capacity. Likewise, many businesses prefer to hire individuals on an as-needed basis, rather than assume the burden of additional employees.

Busy sites such as Guru.com, Elance.com, oDesk.com, and LiveWork .com—a new team-oriented site from virtual outsourcing/call center company LiveOps—provide thriving international marketplaces for talent buyers and talent sellers. In this chapter, we'll introduce you to these and other sites—the "matchmakers"—that can help you open up the gig-spigot as wide as you like.

Bidding: the name of the game

Throughout this book, we refer to jobs and assignments that you can do as a "free agent" (in other words, a freelancer) rather than as an employee, and you'll find many discussed in Chapter 6 and Chapter 12. Here, we'll focus on some of the bigger marketplaces where freelancers can bid on a vast array of projects, and team with other self-employed specialists to take on much larger contracts.

(Keep in mind that bidding can also mean competing with other free-lancers from all over the world, and that fees may not equal what a freelancer might earn from a privately negotiated, non-bid, no-middle-man project. This is why we often suggest that online marketplaces be used to supplement rather than replace a freelancer's private business-development efforts.)

On the freelance hiring side, companies and individuals can generally post projects large and small, of any duration. Freelancers review the particulars and, if they feel they can do the job for suitable compensation, they submit a bid.

The hirer then reviews the bids, comparing qualifications, price, and so forth, and may interview the freelancers who make the preliminary cut, ultimately whittling the list down to the freelancer(s) who can best meet their needs and budget.

We won't get into all the ins and outs here of setting your fees, but in general the "right" fee will:

1. Cover your expenses (project-related as well as a proportionate percentage of your routine overhead).
2. Reflect the value you bring to the project.
3. Provide you a living wage.
4. Include an amount for savings and/or investment in your business.
5. Be competitive with bidders whose value is comparable to yours.

For more detail, you'll find numerous books at Amazon and at public libraries devoted to freelancing, and we ourselves cover it in detail in our book, *The 2-Second Commute: Join the Exploding Ranks of Freelance Virtual Assistants.* We also highly recommend *My So-Called Freelance Life: How to Survive and Thrive as a Creative Professional for Hire* by Michelle Goodman. Michelle gives great advice on freelancing at her blog, too, at anti9to5guide.com.

If you're new to freelance bidding sites, be sure to take your time when you build your profile. This functions as your "resume" for prospective hirers and for fellow freelancers, too, who can be a significant source of both referred and direct work. Set yourself apart by nailing the basics (grammar, punctuation, style, and so forth) and posting a polished and cogent summary of your accomplishments, skills, what makes you an incomparable pleasure to work with, and any testimonials you can lay your hands on (even if it's for that report you proofread for your next-door neighbor).

Most matchmaking sites also allow hirers to rank the freelancer's performance (other metrics may also apply), so always provide excellent service and deliver fully on your commitments. As we all know, positive word-of-mouth rules in the marketplace, just as negative word-of-mouth can quickly sink a freelancer's business.

The major freelance marketplaces

As companies continue to realize the benefits of "as-needed" specialists, and the Internet continues to open up the labor supply—with aging Boomers and younger workers, too, predicted to favor project-based work—freelance numbers and marketplaces can be expected to grow. Following are some of the more important sites where new freelancers can start winning their spurs, and experienced professionals can increase workflow and extend their collaborative networks *ad infinitum.*

Guru.com

When the Internet bubble burst, we watched Guru tweak its business model, adapt, and keep sailing. (The Internet is the Cape Horn of market forces, quickly sending rigid thinking to the bottom of the sea.) In 2003 the site was sold to Indian entrepreneur Inder Guglani, and it has reportedly grown many times over since then.

The site claims more than 100,000 active freelancers, with 56 percent of its members in the United States. It adds, "Guru.com is the world's largest online service marketplace where businesses connect with top freelance talent locally, nationally or globally."

Freelancers can list their services in a variety of categories, including:

◆ Website Design/Website Marketing.

◆ Graphic Design/Presentations/Multimedia.

◆ Illustration/Cartooning/Painting/Sculpting.

◆ Marketing/Advertising/Sales/PR.

◆ Engineering/CAD/Architecture.

◆ Networking/Hardware/Telephone Systems.

◆ Legal.

◆ Fashion/Interior/Landscape/Set Design.

◆ ERP/CRM Implementation.

◆ Programming/Software/Database Development.

- Programming.
- Book Writing/Editing.
- Translation.
- Administrative Support (Legal, Medical, and Accounting).
- Sales/Telemarketing.
- Business Consulting.
- Photography/Videography.
- Finance and Accounting.
- Broadcasting.

Each category also has a set of sub-categories. For example, the Administrative Support category includes:

- Word Processing.
- Data Entry.
- Transcription.
- Event Planning.
- Secretarial Support.
- Office Management.
- HR/Payroll.
- Accounting.
- Paralegal.
- Legal Assistance.
- Medical Billing/Coding.
- Medical Transcription.
- Medical Secretarial Support.

Fees: Freelancer membership options include free registration and several levels of paid membership, which provide additional marketing features. Like Elance and other bidding sites, Guru deducts a commission from the project fee.

Notes: Freelancers new to Guru.com or other matchmaking sites should generally start with the free registration option while they learn the ropes. Later, a paid membership at Guru may be worth the investment (consider it part of your marketing budget), as this reduces the commission rate, though the added marketing options should help build workflow.

If you're new to the process of submitting proposals, Guru provides reference samples, too.

Elance.com

Elance came on the scene in the late 1990s, when entrepreneurs and a few Silicon Valley investors began to see that the Internet might radically accelerate freelance workflow internationally, and that online marketplaces would be the hubs in the wheels. (Like Guru, Elance received substantial venture funding.)

After a few twists and turns (remember what we said about Cape Horn?), Elance is still cranking, posting some 250,000 jobs annually, with a reported value of $100M.

As with Guru, hirers at Elance tap into the freelance talent pool by posting a project and gathering proposals and bids. Once the contract is awarded, the Elance Online Work System enables client and freelancer to communicate for the duration of the project—tracking updates, progress, feedback and more.

Freelancers can list themselves as specialists in Web & Programming, Design & Multimedia, Writing & Translation, Administrative Support, Sales & Marketing, Finance & Management, Legal, and Engineering & Manufacturing. As with Guru, each category embraces a wide range of sub-categories as well.

Fees: Freelancer membership options include free registration and three paid membership plans, with increasing marketing and other features. Elance deducts a commission and other fees from employer payments.

Notes: Similar to Guru, Elance offers an escrow service to hold payment and protect both parties. Dispute-resolution services are also available.

oDesk.com

We've been monitoring oDesk (which reportedly began as "Nodesk"—as in, "freelance from anywhere") off and on since it launched several years ago. At first, its projects skewed heavily toward the tech sector (the company says its biggest category remains Web development), but now the project mix has broadened, and we expect that trend to continue.

oDesk describes itself as "an online staffing marketplace and management platform that provides a convenient way to hire, manage, and pay individuals no matter where they are located."

Besides Web development, projects posted to the site include administrative support, writing, translation, customer service, business services, sales and marketing, networking, information systems, software development, design, and multimedia—in other words, a little something for just about every freelancer.

Fees: Free to join. oDesk collects a commission of 10 percent of the total charge for the project.

Notes: oDesk guarantees payment for hours logged through their system on hourly projects. The site also offers a suite of management and collaboration tools that allow freelancers and hirers to communicate throughout the project. There has been some controversy, however, around oDesk's freelancer-monitoring software, which some say enables hirers to track freelancers' work habits to an intrusive degree.

LiveWork.com

This new freelance team-oriented site comes from LiveOps, an innovative Silicon Valley company that has been known for its virtual call center operations (see Chapter 6), with more than 20,000 home-based agents across the United States. To learn more, we spoke recently with Eckart Walther, senior vice president of LiveOps Marketplace.

Eckart explained that the site is geared toward the rapid assembly of virtual teams of independent contractors ("Experts"), from any location. Teams can take on projects of any size, including those that in the old days might have gone to big "business process outsourcing" (BPO) companies in India, the Philippines, and so forth.

On their sites, LiveOps, LiveWork, and others sometimes refer to such Internet-oriented solutions as "cloudsourcing" (a play on "crowdsourcing"). In the case of work, cloudsourcing means using the Internet (the "cloud") to send—or "source"—projects of any size to workers anywhere, instantly.

LiveWork's key theme is scale: With cloudsourcing (and it bears repeating because of its implications), a virtual project has no outward limits, and can potentially engage thousands of workers internationally. This has long been the promise of virtual work (we sounded a similar theme in our 1999 presentation to the United Nations), and has the potential to deliver significant environmental benefits as well.

Before we move on, a word on site operations. As with other marketplaces, freelancers register and set up their profiles. However, rather than bid on work, they review posted projects, which include proposed pay, and notify hirers where terms are acceptable. Alternatively, Eckart noted, a client can post a project with blank business terms, and Providers (leaders of the virtual companies/teams) can then spell out the terms under which they think they could recruit a team to deliver the work. Many clients aren't sure what per-task compensation would be appropriate, and use this approach.

Fees: Free to join. LiveWork charges a service fee of 10 percent "from the amount paid by the client to the workforce (Expert or Provider) during payment of invoices received."

Notes: The site offers free certification tests for freelancers. LiveWork also offers many project-management communication tools, but does not become involved in adjudicating disputes.

iFreelance.com

iFreelance.com offers a comprehensive marketplace at a very reasonable price. Their tiered membership model (no commissions are charged) lets freelancers find a good fit for their budget and marketing needs, while enabling a robust profile for hirers to review.

Freelancers can list themselves in Accounting/Finance, Administrative Support, Business Consulting, Engineering/Architecture, Graphic Design/Multimedia, Legal, Marketing/Advertising/Sales, Networking/Hardware/Telephony, Traditional Art (Illustration/Painting), Photography/Videography, Programming/Database Development, Training/Education, and Writing/Editing/Translation.

Fees: iFreelance.com has three membership levels: Basic, Silver, and Gold. All are fee-based, but the most expensive is less than $10 per month. They offer discounts for annual memberships.

Notes: Many iFreelance freelancers report building lasting relationships with the clients they meet there. The site's portfolio option also receives high marks from users. (Some feel that this feature alone is worth the low membership fee.)

GetAFreelancer.com

GetAFreelancer.com is a marketplace for buyers and sellers of IT services. Projects require the talents of programmers, Web designers, copywriters, Webmasters, software developers, and similar experts.

Fees: Free to join. Per-project commission of $5 or 10 percent, whichever is higher. Regular uses can opt for a Gold membership, which costs $12 monthly but eliminates commissions.

Notes: Owned by a Swedish company, this site has a distinctly global freelancer mix. You'll be bidding against specialists from India, Romania, Russia, Ukraine, the United States, the U.K., and many other parts of the world.

RentACoder.com

Based in Florida, Rent A Coder, as the name suggests, specializes in custom software projects. But it also includes work for writers, graphic designers, and others.

Fees: Commission of 15 percent of the final bid, with a minimum of $3 for small projects.

Notes: Like other matchmakers, Rent A Coder escrows project funds to protect the parties, and also offers an arbitration process in the event of disputes.

ScriptLance.com

This site, for freelance programmers, is one of the most active of its kind. It's very easy to navigate, and features programming jobs such as PHP, MySQL, Website design, Flash, CSS, Ajax, and many others.

Fees: No registration fees. Straight 5 percent commission on payment for projects, with a $5 minimum.

Notes: On the plus side, many new projects are posted every day. On the minus side, lots of competition. (Also, according to the site's FAQ page, commissions are withheld up front, so you may be billed before you've been paid.)

HotGigs.com

HotGigs is a marketplace for independent consultants. (According to the company, most of the projects are done on-site rather than virtually, so be sure to confirm location requirements before taking on a job.)

Consultant categories include Accounting & Finance, Administrative & Clerical, Business Planning & Management, Compliance & Standards, Creative Design/Media/Writers, Engineering & Design, Environmental & Safety, Healthcare, Human Resources/Recruiting, Information Technology, Insurance, Legal, Manufacturing/Distribution, Marketing & Sales, Music & Artistic, Real Estate/Home, Trainers, Speakers, and Coaches.

Fees: Basic membership is free, though somewhat limited, and Premium membership is available with several payment options. Generally, no commission on projects.

Notes: HotGigs Rate Exchange helps consultants set their rates by viewing what other consultants in their specialty are billing and getting paid.

More freelance project sites to find that juicy gig

- ◆ FreelanceAuction.com—Programmers, IT.
- ◆ CoderTribe.com—Software professionals.
- ◆ FreelanceCentral.net—Print design or Website design.
- ◆ FreelancersOutpost.com—Various, from Administrative to IT.
- ◆ GetACoder.com—Programming and other IT.
- ◆ LimeExchange.com—Various, from Administrative to IT.
- ◆ NoAgenciesPlease.com—IT.
- ◆ Trally.com—Translation and Linguistic.

CHAPTER 12

Making a Little Money on the Side

For some people, full-time or regular part-time work is either not an option or not a preference. They just want to earn a little money on the side. Fortunately, the Internet offers a variety of these opportunities, too.

As you review the choices that follow, you'll see that almost all involve self-employment (aka freelancing) rather than a conventional job. As we point out in Chapter 1, being a "free agent" isn't for everyone, so you'll want to consider your ability and inclination to manage your projects and schedule, and find your next gig.

Get paid to answer questions

If you've often found yourself thinking, "If I had a dime for every time I've answered that question, I'd be rich!" then these sites might be just the thing.

As you scroll through the list, you'll see references here and there in our Notes to a "minimum payout." This refers to the minimum earnings you must accumulate in your account before you can get paid.

AQA 63336 and AQA2U (aqa.63336.com)

AQA (Any Question Answered) 63336 is a U.K.-based service that works with researchers in the United States, Canada, Ireland, Australia, New Zealand, and South Africa. Researchers get paid to answer questions via computer from users in the U.K. and Ireland. (A new service, AQA2U, pays experts to text messages to "fans and followers." Experts must have access to a U.K. mobile phone.)

Notes: Applicants for research positions must pass a test; pay-per-action; reputation for insisting on high quality.

BitWine (bitwine.com)

BitWine enables online experts to provide advice in various fields including nutrition, travel, technology, business, spirituality, and so on. Users consult with experts virtually via Skype's VoIP technology.

Notes: Experts set their own fees and pay 20 to 25 percent commission to BitWine.

ChaCha (chacha.com)

ChaCha, another quick-information service, contracts with home-based workers for several "Guide Roles." These include Expeditors, Generalists, Specialists, and Transcribers.

Expediters standardize and categorize incoming questions, then route them to the best available Guides. *Generalists* are Internet researchers who quickly look up answers to user questions in a wide variety of categories. *Specialists* answer questions in specific areas. *Transcribers* listen to recordings of questions called in by users and then convert the questions into text.

Notes: Pays monthly, with a minimum payout of $100; lesser amounts roll over into next month; payment via transfer to U.S. bank account or credit to a debit card; pay-per-action.

JustAnswer (justanswer.com)

JustAnswer works with highly qualified experts in numerous subject areas. When users post questions, they specify the fee they're willing to pay for the answer and deposit that amount with JustAnswer. Experts receive 25 to 50 percent of that amount, based on their experience and approval rating.

Notes: Paid on acceptance of answer; minimum payout $20; payment via PayPal.

kgb (kgb.com)

kgb (Knowledge Generation Bureau) works with home-based "Special Agents" who answer questions texted in by users. Questions run the gamut. (For example, Chris was browsing recently in a sprawling used-book market, and couldn't remember the author of the science fiction novel, *Dune*. She texted her question to kgbkgb, authorized a 99-cent charge to her phone, and in less than 30 seconds received a text with the answer: Frank Herbert.)

Notes: Must pass a test to work with company; pay-per-action.

Weegy (weegy.com)

"Weegy" is an artificial being who engages users in a "problem-solving conversation" and taps into an advanced search engine for answers. When Weegy can't answer the user's question, "she" calls on the expertise of a live "Weegy Expert."

Notes: Minimum payout $20; pay-per-action.

Get paid to take surveys

Although it's true there are many scams in the "paid survey" sector (don't ever pay to participate in surveys, and you should steer clear of those that require you to register for "offers" beforehand), there are legitimate opportunities as well. You won't make a bundle, but surveys can provide a steady flow of extra cash if you take them often.

Bear in mind that you may not qualify to participate in every survey. Each survey comes with its own "target market" requirements, and survey companies select users on that basis. For example, a survey involving anti-aging facial cream might be open exclusively to women between the ages of 35 and 55.

To the same end, legitimate survey companies may ask you to provide demographic information about yourself and others living in your home during the registration process.

To get you started, here are some survey sites we've heard great things about.

Company/URL	Payment/Compensation Information
ACOP.com	Compensation may be monetary or in merchandise; brief "screener" surveys determine who is eligible for more comprehensive surveys.
ClearVoiceSurveys.com	Pays in points that can be redeemed for cash, gift certificates, or merchandise.
GlobalTestMarket.com	Pays in points redeemable for cash.
HBS.edu/cler	Harvard Business School Computer Lab for Experimental Research pays from $15 to $40 per study; compensation may be cash or electronic gift certificates for well-known online stores.
HCDSurveys.com	Pays in points redeemable for cash or gift certificates.
i-Say.com	Ipsos i-Say pays with points redeemable for merchandise or gift cards.
LightspeedPanel.com	Earn points redeemable for cash, online gift certificates, prizes.
MySurvey.com	Pays in points redeemable for cash, charity donations, or merchandise.
NielsenNetPanel.com	Pays in cash or merchandise rewards.
OpinionOutpost.com	Pays in points redeemable for cash, gift certificates, or other rewards.
PineconeResearch.com	Pays $3 per survey, with opportunities to try products before they are available in stores.
SurveySpot.com	Cash payments and chances to win prizes.
ValuedOpinions.com	Pays in gift certificates when your account reaches $20.
Your2Cents.com	Pays in points redeemable for cash when your account reaches $10.

Get paid to mystery shop

Contrary to our heading (and popular belief), mystery shoppers don't actually "get paid to shop," but rather to file reports containing their feedback on a shopping experience.

For example, a mystery shopper might be instructed to do a "shop" at the local branch of a donut chain. There, she'll order certain items—let's say a donut and a medium coffee—and assess their quality. She'll also make mental notes (because writing actual notes would take the "mystery" out of mystery shopping) about the cleanliness of the establishment, the courtesy and appearance of the staff, and so on. After she files her report, she'll be reimbursed the cost of the items she bought, and receive a small fee (usually between $5 and $9 for a "shop" of this kind).

Unfortunately, scammers have jumped on the mystery shopping bandwagon, too, so be sure to keep two things in mind when you look for this type of work:

1. Real mystery shopping companies do not charge a fee to work with them. They typically make their money from the companies their shoppers report on.
2. Legitimate mystery shopping companies will never send you large checks and ask you to wire money back to them. Because this is such a common scam, we repeat: *never.*

Here are 25 legitimate mystery shopping companies you might want to consider. We also maintain a list of sites at RatRaceRebellion.com, and you'll find a great list at Volition.com, too.

Company	Website
A&A Merchandising	aamerch.com
A Closer Look	a-closer-look.com
Ardent Services	ardentservices.com
Beyond Marketing Group	beyondmarketinggroup.com
CheckMark	checkmarkinc.com
Customer Impact	customerimpactinfo.com
Focus On Service	focusonservice.com
ICC/Decision Services	iccds.com
IntelliShop	intelli-shop.com
Market Viewpoint	marketviewpoint.com
Mystery Guest	mysteryguestinc.com
Mystery Shoppers	mystery-shoppers.com

Premier Service	premierservice.ca
Quality Shopper	qualityshopper.org
Rentrak	ms.rentrak.com
Restaurant Cops	restaurant-cops.com
Ritter Associates	ritterandassociates.com
Second to None	second-to-none.com
Service Alliance	servicellianceinc.com
Service Performance Group	spgweb.com
Service Research Corporation	serviceresearch.com
ServiceSleuth	servicesleuth.com
Shoppers, Inc.	shopperjobs.com
Spies in Disguise	spiesindisguise.com
Video Eyes	videoeyes.net

Get paid to test new ideas: participating in focus groups

In addition to surveys, companies and other organizations can get answers to marketing and similar questions through focus groups. Participants may answer questions or participate in discussions about products, services, messages, concepts, advertisements, packaging, and so forth.

Back in the day, focus-group research took take place face-to-face, with participants gathered in one location. Now, companies can gather their input online or by telephone, giving you an excellent way to earn extra money at home.

Following is a list of hirers of virtual focus-group participants, with a brief description of the hirer in its own words.

20/20 Research (2020research.com)

"20/20 Research is in the business of conducting market research, the results of which are used to improve products and services. Our company provides a way for you, as consumers, to make your thoughts and opinions known to the corporations that provide services and create products that you use every day."

ABILITY Panel (abilitypanel.com)

"ABILITY is a group of online panels for people with disabilities, their family members, advocates, and other stakeholders. Participants in our research have the opportunity to make their voices heard by participating in groundbreaking Market Research, Mystery Shopping, Surveys, and other specialized studies."

AlphaBuzz (alphabuzzgroup.com)

"We aggressively maintain and grow our nationwide database, keeping it dynamic, up-to-date, clean, and targeted to provide you with fresh, articulate, and charismatic respondents, comprehensively tracked, to ensure new participants for all your research."

e-FocusGroups (e-focusgroups.com)

"We maintain an online panel, i.e., a database of individuals who would like to earn money for their participation in online focus groups and/or surveys. Every respondent who participates in one of our online focus groups gets paid (amount varies depending on requirements of the project)."

FindFocusGroups (findfocusgroups.com)

"FindFocusGroups.com uses many different online sources to find out about upcoming studies, including direct information from market research companies, and then passes this info on to you. The FindFocusGroups .com database allows you to find focus groups by country, state, city, category, etc."

Focus Forward Online (focusfwdonline.com)

"Focus Forward Online is a leader in the online market research industry. By using cutting edge web based and back-end technology, Focus Forward Online allows companies to improve their products and services by learning more about their customers' needs and preferences."

Hagen/Sinclair (hagensinclair.com)

"We are always looking for qualified individuals to take part in paid research studies. Studies cover a diversity of topics and include professional, political and consumer opportunities."

Get paid to see the future

Are you intuitive, psychic, spiritual, or otherwise qualified to offer insights into the future? If so, there are companies who would like to hear from you (but you probably already knew that!).

Most phone psychics find success through positive word-of-mouth (customer referrals), so a warm and caring attitude will go a long way toward building your reputation and client base. Phone psychics are typically paid per minute on the phone with clients.

Company	Website
Circle of Stars	circleofstars.com
Guiding Light	guidinglightpsychics.com
PsychicsNeeded	psychicsneeded.com
Serenity's Northern New Age	serenity-snna.com
Whispy	whispy.com

Get paid to write

Whether you're submitting articles for specific Websites or for mass distribution, or you're blogging for yourself or someone else, writing can be an excellent way to bring home the bacon. What you earn will depend largely on how much or how often you write, the quality of your work, and, increasingly, your marketing efforts.

We've already highlighted some job sites for writers in Chapter 6, and will round them out here with some excellent resources for bloggers.

Though it's possible to make an excellent living as a blogger (some well-known bloggers such as Darren Rowse, at problogger.net, and Steve Pavlina, at stevepavlina.com, earn six-figure incomes), it's rare. But many bloggers make modest, supplemental incomes. Blogging positions typically pay by the post, or a share of ad revenues generated by the blog, or both.

451 Press (451press.com)

There are two pages on this site that you'll want to check—"Jobs" and "Write for us." The first lists pay-per-post job openings and topics that are available now; the second details the site's revenue-share blogging model.

b5media (b5media.com)

Cofounded by Aussie blogging expert Darren Rowse (who also works at home), b5media maintains hundreds of blogs covering a wide array of topics. Its jobs are posted to ProBlogger.net's blogging-jobs board. (See ProBlogger.net in this section.)

Content Quake (contentquake.com)

The Content Quake tagline—"Individual Bloggers Making a Collective Difference"—sums up their mission. This community of bloggers covers many subjects and uses a pay-per-post compensation model.

Families.com

As the name suggests, Families.com covers topics relating to family, home, parenting, and relationships. Click the "Blog For Us!" link at the bottom of the home page for blogger specifications. Pay is per post and increases through time, with bonuses "based on performance."

ProBlogger (problogger.net)

One of our favorites, Rat Race Rebellion researchers visit this site every day. In addition to blogging jobs from around the Internet, the owner, Darren Rowse, shares vast amounts of information and expertise on blogging topics. If you're serious about succeeding as a blogger, this is a "Must Bookmark" site.

Review Me (reviewme.com)

For writers with their own blogs, Review Me offers an opportunity to write paid reviews of products and services from various companies. (Similar sites include blogsvertise.com and sponsoredreviews.com.)

WriteBite (writebite.com)

If you're a ranter, debater, or just have strong opinions, WriteBite could be a great platform for pontification. Only the most popular rants of the week get a payout, but we all need a place to blow off steam, right?

If you have a blog of your own (or plan to), check the following sites for various advertising options to "monetize" (make money with) it.

◆ smorty.com

◆ shopzilla.com

◆ azoogleads.com

◆ adbrite.com

◆ cj.com

◆ bidclix.com

◆ google.com/adsense

◆ affiliate-program.amazon.com

◆ chitika.com

◆ widgetbucks.com

Get paid to perform various tasks

Because home-based work is such a hodgepodge, every book about it needs hodgepodge sections, and this is one of ours. Here you'll find mini-gigs ranging from voice-mail transcription to getting paid to review Websites.

Amazon Mechanical Turk (mturk.com)

Amazon Mechanical Turk is a marketplace that coordinates computer programs and human intelligence to perform tasks posted by "requestors." As an "MTurk," you complete HITs (Human Intelligence Tasks) that might include finding the e-mail addresses of certain professors, taking surveys, rating the relevance of a Website's content to its domain name, writing articles, and so forth. Tasks can usually be done quickly. Pay typically ranges from a few cents to a few dollars, depending on the task's complexity, with some paying $20 or more.

Notes: Minimum payout $10; payment via transfer to U.S. bank account, or credit to an Amazon.com gift certificate; pay-per-action.

Miles of Marketing (milesofmarketing.com)

We've heard great things about Miles of Marketing. This moms-only opportunity involves two-week promotion campaigns in which reps help spread the word about a given product. Promotional activities include driving with a magnetic decal on your car, distributing samples, talking about the product to friends, and so on. Reps file a report at the end of the campaign.

Notes: Pay is per completed marketing cycle.

Movie Standee Installers (standeejobs.com)

Anyone who goes to the movies is familiar with those big stand-up displays in the lobby for current and "coming soon" films. Perhaps you assumed (as we did) that cinema staff put them up, but it's often done by independent contractors. In this work *from* home (as opposed to *at* home) position, the company sends you the unassembled displays, and you transport them to the assigned theaters, assemble them, and send the company a photo of the finished product through your cell phone.

Notes: You'll need a larger vehicle (such as an SUV or minivan) to transport the display boxes.

Pixazza (pixazza.com)

Pixazza experts match online photos of products with products offered by Pixazza affiliates. The result is a graphic-based advertisement that will be placed on sites across the Internet.

Notes: Pay is per item tagged, plus a commission on every transaction to purchase an item you identified.

Quicktate (quicktate.com)

Quicktate uses home-based transcribers to turn client voice-mail messages and personal notes into written form. We've seen the people who transcribe for Quicktate refer to themselves as "Quicktaters" on some of the work-at-home forums, and they seem to be quite happy with the work.

Notes: Pay is per word; company also hires bilingual Spanish/English transcribers.

ShortTask (shorttask.com)

This site offers a matching service for "Seekers" (people who need to have a task completed) and "Solvers" (those who provide assistance). Similar to the Amazon Mechanical Turk model, tasks are posted by Seekers along with the "reward" they are willing to pay for their completion.

Notes: Minimum payout $50; Seekers prepay for tasks and funds are transferred to Solver's account when Seeker approves performance.

TicketPuller (ticketpuller.com)

We've heard from many people who are making money and having fun working as "ticket pullers." Ticket pullers have to type fast and know how to get around the Internet, as they have to secure "hot" tickets as soon as they go on sale. They dive into the online buying frenzy, and pluck the best tickets they can. (Don't worry, pullers don't use their own credit cards, but buy through the company's account with the ticket outlets.)

Notes: Pay depends on the success of your pulling session, and is based on a percentage of the ticket cost

UserTesting.com

Website owners often wonder what the user experience is like for people visiting their sites for the first time. As a UserTesting "website user," you'll give them candid, as-it-happens feedback as you view their site. UserTesting's software records what's happening on your screen as you offer your reactions vocally by microphone or telephone.

Notes: Pay is $10 per test completed in accordance with the instructions.

Get paid to pass judgment

The Internet has changed many professions, including how some attorneys prepare for jury trials. Now, through services such as those listed here, lawyers can test their cases with home-based "mock jurors" (instead of having them assemble in a room, as in the old days) before going "live" in court.

Compensation varies from case to case, depending on the complexity of the material that the e-jurors are asked to review. (Bonus tip: Though anyone fitting the stated criteria can register to be an e-juror, these sites often have more women than men in their databases. This makes them a ripe opportunity for men, to round out the jury pools.)

◆   eJury (ejury.com)

◆   JuryTest (jurytest.com)

◆   OnlineVerdict.com

Get paid to be creative

There was a time when selling your artwork on T-shirts, mugs, mouse pads, or other items meant paying a setup fee and investing in inventory.

Now, a number of Websites let you create, sell, and profit for free. In fact, you can set up an online store at no cost to promote your products.

Simply create your images and upload them to the site. Select the merchandise you'd like to put your image on (there are dozens of items to choose from: clothes, clocks, bumper stickers, books, and so forth), set your price, and go! These services print to order, handle all billing, shipping, and returns, and cut you a check for your profits at the end of each month.

◆ CafePress (cafepress.com)

◆ Zazzle (zazzle.com)

◆ Printfection (printfection.com)

◆ Spreadshirt (spreadshirt.com)

For crafters and artists the Internet offers an expanding array of outlets for showcasing and selling your work.

Company/URL	Details
Art Fire artfire.com	A marketplace and community for artists and buyers of handmade items. Fees: Free for the basic option; upgraded options available.
crowdSPRING crowdspring.com	A venue where buyers post creative projects they need to have done (for example, "logo needed"), along with the fee they'll pay, and artists from around the world propose solutions. The buyer picks the one he or she likes best and awards the job. The site handles creative work of every sort, including Web design, logos, illustration, stationery design, multimedia, package graphics, clothing, ad banners, blog themes, product design, photography, and more. Fees: No fees for creatives.
DaWanda.com (France, U.K., Germany) dawanda.com	A marketplace where crafters and artisans can sell handmade and related products. Fees: 5 percent commission on item sales price.

eBay ebay.com	eBay can be an excellent platform for selling handmade items. The site has a "Crafts Selling Guide" for crafters of all kinds. Fees: Listing fees only.
Etsy etsy.com	Some of our favorite crafters swear by Etsy. The site connects buyers with creators of a wide range of handmade items, vintage goods, and supplies. Fees: A modest listing fee, plus a 3.5 percent transaction fee on items sold.
SmashingDarling smashingdarling.com	Set up an online boutique (or several) at this fashion-focused site, and sell your unique clothing and accessories. Fees: Free to set up; 18 percent transaction fee on all sales.
Threadless threadless.com	Our favorite T-shirt site. "A community-based tee shirt company with an ongoing, open call for design submissions." Artists submit designs; community votes; winning designs earn cash and other prizes.

Get paid to be artificial

If you've ever wanted to be someone else and fly around in a weird world and make friends (gee, who hasn't?)—and earn some money, too—now's your chance. The Internet is a growing platform for artificial beings in artificial worlds (with gigantic environments like MapleStory hosting the younger generations), and even a few real-life millionaires have emerged from these make-believe societies.

Liaison, host, or event coordinator

It may sound odd, but at any given moment, tens of thousands of people (millions more, if you count game sites such as World of Warcraft) are logged into Internet-based worlds. In the form of artificial beings called "avatars," they explore their new environments (and get lost), open and run stores, buy clothes, speculate in real estate, hang out in bars and clubs, attend college courses and corporate presentations, and much more. (Be warned, though, that as in the real world, some parts can be a bit "edgy.")

To manage and facilitate all this activity, the companies who maintain these artificial worlds periodically hire "in-world" event hosts, liaisons, greeters, community managers, and so on, who can work at home. Sites where these positions sometimes pop up include:

◆ Second Life (lindenlab.com)

◆ There (there.com)

As mentioned, entrepreneurs are also operating stores and other businesses in these online worlds, selling virtual goods and services for real money. For example, not long ago we interviewed "Boshemia," the online name of a Colorado woman who runs a store in Second Life, where she personalizes avatars for customers. Working from home, Boshemia told us she expects to make approximately $10,700 profit this year. (For more on Boshemia, see her blog at sugarpatch.com.)

It's hard to predict where the Internet will take us next—the good, the bad, the who-knows-what—but one thing is for sure: It will be an interesting ride.

CHAPTER 13

Your Telework Resume and Interview

Unearthing that ideal job lead is great, but it comes to naught without a strong resume and interview skills to get the offer. In our years of helping people find and land home-based jobs, we've had many conversations with HR managers and other decision makers tasked with reviewing resumes, conducting interviews, and extending job offers. Here, we'll share with you some of the tips we've gathered from experts and job seekers alike.

Does a telework resume really need to be different?

In a word, yes. There are three key reasons why work-at-home resumes require a different mindset and approach.

1. **Stiffer competition.** Because in most specialties the demand for legitimate home-based jobs far exceeds the supply, job ads often generate floods of applications. Bear in mind, too, that in the telework arena you're often competing not only with local applicants, but regional, national, and even international job seekers as well.

2. **Telework resumes are critiqued more harshly than others.** Given the abundance of resumes for virtual positions,

hirers can afford to be extremely picky about whom they interview and hire.

Managers of home-based work teams also know that experience in a specialty or field, by itself, doesn't guarantee that the applicant can succeed in a remote-work situation. Rather, they're looking for the right mix of experience, skills, accomplishments, character traits, and home-office arrangements. Applicants who don't make those qualities stand out in their resumes are unlikely to hear back from the company.

3. **You can't count on compensating for a mediocre resume with a dazzling interview.** If your charm, charisma, and winning smile were your "secret weapons" in job hunts past, you're in a new game now. In many cases, telework interviews are conducted over the phone rather than face-to-face. This means that job seekers accustomed to relying on charm and other physical factors to offset mediocre resumes will need a new plan.

Telework resume bravos and blunders

To recap, getting that home-based job may require an overhaul of your resume, your interview techniques, and your mindset. Following are some resume bravos and blunders to keep in mind as you write (or rewrite) your resume.

Bravos

1. **Create a list of position- and experience-related "keywords" to include in your resume.** Many employers are now using software that scans resumes for desired keywords before human eyes ever see them. Be sure to consider the keywords a target employer is likely to be scanning for and include them in your resume.

The job listing itself can be an excellent source of keywords. Read the job description carefully and blend some of the hirer's own keywords into your resume.

You can incorporate keywords either by including a "Keywords" section (adding it to the usual "Objectives," "Employment History," "Education," and so forth), or by sprinkling the keywords in appropriate places in the resume's text.

2. **Increase or update certifications wherever advanta-geous.** It goes without saying that certifications in key skill areas can keep you in the running or help set you apart. One of our favorite online assessment and certification resources is BrainBench.com. Though not meant to stand in for a Harvard MBA, BrainBench does offer hundreds of inexpensive certifications that can help bolster a resume quickly and conveniently. (These can be particularly useful if you've been out of the workforce for a while.)

3. **Don't rely solely on your word processor's spell-check feature for the final proofread.** Spell check is great, but don't let it have the final word on something as important as your resume. Instead, have a sharp-eyed friend or family member, or a resume expert, review your resume for proper spelling and grammar.

4. **Focus on your skills, accomplishments, and traits rather than "home."** The employer already knows the job will be home-based, so there's no need to linger on that aspect of the position (as some job seekers are inclined to do). Instead, focus on the skills, achievements, and traits that demonstrate your ability to excel in the position you're applying for and to work independently.

Blunders

For a specialist's view, we asked professional resume writer and career strategist Jennifer Anthony (JennWrites.com) to share the three biggest "blunders" she sees job seekers make when writing their telework resumes. Here's what she had to say.

In my experience, there are very common resume mistakes (e.g., spelling errors) that I have observed from entry-level workers to executives. However, telecommuters seem to be plagued with three specific blunders that can ruin their chances of getting an interview.

1. Including personal information. This is the most common error that telecommuters make. Your objective statement should not indicate that you would like to work from home just so you don't have to pay for daycare costs. It sounds incredibly unprofessional, and it is not information your potential employer needs to know. It is well known that most

teleworkers are parents, but it is assumed that you will have the proper childcare in place. The same rule applies to your marital status, your religious beliefs, and your financial status. There is no reason to add anything in your resume that could disqualify you.

2. Writing a self-centered objective statement. The objective statement has been a pet peeve of mine for a long time. The reason why is that most job seekers write something generic and self-centered that doesn't address what they have to offer a company. Writing something like "looking for a stable company with good benefits and potential for growth" can sound a bit like an attitude. Instead, use a headline followed by a compelling skills summary demonstrating what skills you have to offer your potential employer.

3. Sending the wrong file format. If the job ad asks for a resume to be sent in Word, don't send a Works or Illustrator file and expect it to be opened. Additionally, you must learn how to create a plain-text resume file that you can copy and paste into Web forms and e-mail. You can't just copy and paste out of your Word file, because it will not format correctly.

Prepare your resume in 3 formats

Expanding on Jennifer's last recommendation, we suggest you prepare and save your resume in three formats. This will help you respond quickly and effectively when you spot that perfect job lead.

Traditional Word resume

Because Microsoft Word is the most common word-processing application for both job seekers and hirers, we recommend using it for your conventional format. If you don't have Word, however, use the alternative you have on hand, and save the document as a Rich Text Format (RTF) file with your computer's "save as" feature. (RTF functions as a universal word processor language, and can be read by hirers with PCs or Macs, and with most word-processing applications.)

In Word or RTF, your resume can also easily be converted into a PDF file using free services such as PDFOnline.com and FreePDFConvert.com.

When to use this format: Use this option when you're asked to send your resume via conventional mail, fax, or e-mail attachment (unless, of course, another format such as PDF or plain text is specified).

Plain text or ASCII text resume

As Jennifer pointed out, a resume in Word typically cannot be cut and pasted into Web-based job-application forms and e-mail. Instead, you need to use "plain text." A plain text or ASCII (American Standard Code for Information Interchange) text resume removes all those special characters (bullets, tabs, text boxes, graphics, and so on) and formatting attributes (bold, underline, italics, and so forth) that can be muddled or twisted into gibberish on the receiving end.

To create a plain text resume, most people simply convert their Word resume by clicking on "File" at the top of the page, then choosing "Save as," then selecting "Plain text (.txt)" from the drop-down "Save as type" menu.

But the cleanest way to convert your resume to an ASCII text format is to copy and paste it into Microsoft Notepad (not Wordpad). Notepad not only removes all customized formatting automatically, but it also won't allow users to add special characters back into the document.

You can dress up your plain text resume by using BLOCK CAPS where you would have used bold, asterisks in place of bullet points, dashed lines instead of text boxes, and so forth.

When to use this format: The plain text or ASCII resume should be used when you're asked to submit your resume in the body of an e-mail or via an online form, or when a plain text resume is requested as an e-mail attachment.

Online/HTML resume

Although it's generally not a must, an online resume (that is, your resume on a Web page) can be a good way to distinguish yourself from other candidates and show hirers your comfort with technology.

Online resumes are particularly useful for freelancers, who can insert links to online portfolios or other work. For example, Web designers can link to sites they've designed, bloggers to posts they've made, and graphic artists to samples of their logos.

When to use this format: In addition to the examples just mentioned, job seekers can include the URL (Web address) of an online resume in correspondence to prospective employers. It can also facilitate networking, as the simple Web address can be shared and forwarded more easily than the entire resume.

Using "power words" to amp up your telework resume

Regardless of their job descriptions, the majority of teleworkers share certain characteristics, and you'll want to find the best way to convey them in your resume. These traits—many of which are valued in employees across the board—include:

◆ Initiative.

◆ Problem-solving skills.

◆ Organizational skills (time, tasks, and priorities).

◆ Project management skills.

◆ Discipline.

◆ Sets and achieves goals.

◆ Computer literacy.

◆ Ability to balance attention between major objectives and details.

◆ Excellent communications skills, written and oral.

◆ Ability to work effectively with little or no supervision.

◆ Accountable for work quality, productivity, and so on.

◆ Follows directions precisely.

As you construct your resume, choose the traits you possess, then give some thought to words (typically verbs) and phrasing that might convey most effectively how you've applied these characteristics in your work to date. (Remember to stick to the facts. If you claim to possess a certain skill or trait, the interviewer may well ask for an example of how you've used it in your work. Never make false claims in your resume; lies have a way of leading to embarrassment, humiliation, or worse.)

Injecting your resume with action or power words (and avoiding flat or passive language) can bring to life in the reader's mind your capabilities and character, and your fitness for the job. For example, consider how simple changes can create a very different image:

Changed the way the assembly line worked to improve overall efficiency.

or

Evaluated assembly line processes and implemented streamlined methods, boosting output by 43%.

The second statement employs power words—*evaluated, implemented, streamlined, boosting*—which not only vivify your profile and experience, but convey valuable teleworker traits such as initiative and self-actualization, and setting and achieving goals. (And as experienced resume-writers know, including specifics—such as "43%" in the example—sharpens the overall statement, conveys attention to detail, and makes the reader more confident of the claim's validity.)

Examples of Power Words

accomplished	qualified	determined
expanded	reduced	obtained
empowered	enhanced	formulated
invented	supervised	conceptualized
updated	compiled	documented
decreased	won	persuaded
represented	discovered	improved
completed	systematized	produced
presented	implemented	consulted
built	quantified	constructed
performed	coordinated	negotiated
generated	convinced	evaluated
initiated	operated	created
increased	proposed	adapted
promoted	controlled	provided
managed	simplified	devised
compared	advised	planned
organized	streamlined	restored
overhauled	detected	established
budgeted	analyzed	influenced
processed	executed	assisted
eliminated	delivered	corrected
identified	headed	conducted
founded	guided	developed
exceeded	solved	achieved
recognized	scheduled	prepared

In the following sample resume, provided by our guest resume expert Jennifer Anthony, you'll see how Jennifer puts power/action words to use, highlights characteristics found among successful teleworkers, focuses on skills and accomplishments, and has carefully checked the spelling and grammar in her document.

JENN JOBSEEKER jenn@jennwrites.com	555 Street Address City, ST 12345 Home: 555-555-1234 Cell: 555-555-4321

EXPERTISE	**Telecommute Professional:**
• Medical Terminology • Medical Billing Experience • Medical & Legal Transcription Experience • Confidential Recordkeeping • Type 90 WPM • Microsoft Office Expert • WordPerfect Expert • WAV Pedal • Express Scribe • Instant Text • FTP / Internet • Browsers	**Medical Transcription/Medical Billing Specialist** Experienced ~ Team Player ~ Computer Savvy ~ Quick Learner Highlights: Expert English grammar and spelling skills. Able to prepare accurate and concise documents in a prompt manner to meet strict deadlines. Strong computer literacy and quick study of new technology. Over 2,000 audio hours of medical transcription logged, including both clinical and acute care reports. • Mature professional looking to utilize 20+ years of experience to transition into a medical transcription or medical billing career from a remote office. • Detail-oriented and highly self-motivated, known for going the extra mile and consistently exceeding employer and customer expectations. • Proven ability to work positively under pressure and adapt quickly to new roles, and challenges.

EDUCATION **Medical Transcription Certificate,** 2003 College Name **Microsoft Office Certification,** 1998 College Name	CAREER PROGRESSION COMPANY NAME – City, ST **Transcriptionist** (100% telecommute), 3/2008 to Present • Transcribe, edit, and proofread medical digital audio files. • Known for fast turn around time and high accuracy rates. INSURANCE COMPANY NAME – City, ST **Office Manager/Biller/Data Entry**, 3/1998 to 12/2008 *Promoted three times during my tenure at Company Name.* • Processed claims for workers' compensation and entered bills into database. • Prepared documents to be sent to underwriters for approval. • Verified policies for accuracy and completeness and updated operator instructions as necessary. • Created training manuals and trained other team members. • Developed, implemented, and promoted strategies to achieve significant profit increases. COUNTY COURT NAME – City, ST **Court Recorder / Legal Assistant** (to Judge), 3/1989 to 2/1998 • Recorded and transcribed criminal and civil hearings and trials. • Drafted and typed all jury charges and motion rulings and organized and distributed jury duty summons. • Acted as liaison between attorneys and judge regarding status of motions and other pending litigation. • Organized and maintained judge's files of pending suits and managed all correspondence.

The telework interview: employers' and our favorite tips

Preparing for a telework interview is similar to getting ready for a conventional interview, with the primary difference depending on whether the interview will be entirely by phone. Following are some pointers—first a few of our own favorites, then tips from employers—to help you do your best.

◆ Concentrate on conveying your value to the company, rather than the value of teleworking to you. Many people want to spend more time with their children, eliminate their commutes, or care for elders. These are all laudable goals, but they are yours rather than the company's. The company's goal is to make a profit—through the "assets" of people like you.

◆ Be polite, courteous, and professional in *all* your dealings with the employer, from the first e-mail to the last thank-you. (Needless to add, this includes administrative staff, whose influence on personnel decisions of all kinds should never be underestimated. Your goal should be to leave strong, positive impressions all along the line.)

Employers themselves had these tips to share:

◆ "Treat the interview as if it were face-to-face. Even though you're at home, put on business clothes, find a quiet place to talk, be prepared, have your notes handy."
—Jonathan Means, senior vice president and general manager, Kelly Services, Inc. (KellyConnect®)

◆ "Thoroughly research the company and the position you are applying for prior to the interview. Prepare a list of questions to ask during the interview and also review responses to questions you anticipate the interviewer will ask you. Prior to the telephone interview, determine a quiet, distraction-free place to conduct the phone call, as you would in a typical face-to-face interview. The interview is meant to test your ability to be attentive, focused, and friendly over the phone. Use the opportunity to demonstrate your knowledge of the company and your interest in contributing to its success."
—Donna Neale, vice president, Contact Center Operations, *NEW*

◆ "Provide information for an objective assessment so you and your manager can make an informed decision on whether a remote work arrangement will work for you and for the organization. Come prepared to discuss your work profile, work arrangement preferences, and any organizational support required to make the work arrangement successful, such as:

> ◆ The ability to access your work resources from anywhere, amount of your communication with others that is done over the network vs. face to face, ability to measure your work outputs or results....

> ◆ Your remote work style, self-management skills, communication expectations, technical resourcefulness, home-to-office commute time....

> ◆ Support—Is your home (or other) environment conducive to working away from the office, can you remotely access needed technology, are your manager and team supportive of you working remotely?"

—Heidi Pate, senior product marketing manager, Open Work Services Group, Sun Microsystems

◆ "(1) Show up on time, (2) be articulate, (3) be friendly, (4) know your work history, (5) shut down or remove any background noise, and (6) stay on topic with responses."
—Gayle Buske, cofounder, president, and CEO, Team Double-Click

Because many job seekers are interested in the growing field of online teaching, we also sought interview advice from Dr. Dani Babb, online teaching expert and author of the popular guides *Make Money Teaching Online* and *The Accidental Startup*, at drdaniellebabb.com. Dani had these tips to share:

> "Be prepared with answers to the following questions:
> 1. Why teach online?
> 2. How is online teaching different from brick-and-mortar education? Be familiar with the drastically different demographics in online universities, the individual's choice to go to school rather than being 'forced' by parents, and so on.
> 3. What is your graduate specialty, and how does that align with what you want to teach online?

4.   How do you create interest and keep students focused without seeing them face to face?

5.   Why is responsiveness important in an online environment?

6.   What tools do you use to help communicate with students?"

Employer follow-up is changing

Not so long ago, job seekers who had submitted a resume or been interviewed for a position could expect a polite letter on quality bond, informing them of their status. In today's hurried (and resume-swamped) world, however, many HR managers have adopted a policy of "We'll contact you if you're selected."

For the job seeker, this new practice can be extremely frustrating, and even more demoralizing than the written rejection days, because the silence can feed feelings of insignificance, anonymity, and desperation.

Our advice? At the end of the interview, ask when it's expected that a decision will be made, and if you may follow up if you haven't heard anything within a certain (reasonable) time. Try to be patient with the system (joblessness and financial pressure never make this easy), and keep multiple job irons in the fire, to reduce the feeling that everything rides on one position or decision.

Now let's get some parting advice from women and men who are walking the talk across the United States, successfully working from home.

CHAPTER 14

Tips From the Trenches

In our final chapter, we wanted you to hear directly from successful home-based workers as they share their most effective tips, techniques, and tools for making home-based work work.

Dealing with naysayers

Tipster: Calissa Hatton has been working from home as a freelance writer and virtual assistant since 1999.

"Some people, family and friends, might laugh or make you feel silly for taking on a work-at-home job. It can make you feel very alone just starting out. Find an online community that you can go to for support. There are many message boards for those who work at home, and they can be a source of advice, including how to deal with family and friends who don't take your job seriously.

You can tell those who discourage you how much money you are making, or perhaps note the company you work for (Google, Apple, Barnes & Noble, etc.). Don't forget to mention the fact that you don't have to get up early, commute to work, deal with coworkers or bosses. That usually gets them asking, 'How can I do that?'"

Authors' note: There will always be people who act as thouhg home-based work is not a "real job." We just chalk it up to "slipper envy," and count ourselves lucky that we're not in a traditional office with them!

Managing time, tasks, and priorities

Tipster: Calissa Hatton has been working from home as a freelance writer and virtual assistant since 1999.

"Simplify your time by limiting how much you spend checking e-mails. Only check e-mails once or twice a day. It's a hard habit to break if you're used to checking your e-mail every five minutes, or when the computer dings. Close your e-mail when you aren't using it. Once you are checking your e-mail, devote yourself. Don't multitask with phone calls or other things. If there is an emergency, add an auto-responding e-mail and have people call a special phone line dedicated to emergencies. Try this trick with phone calls as well.

"Many people who work from home often have more than one job, just in case one opportunity should fall through. When you have more than one job, and you're struggling to figure out which one should be given priority, consider your hourly rate. If you can make $15 an hour at a call center, but you make $18 an hour with a transcription job, give the majority of your hours to your transcription work, and do the minimal hours for the call center."

Tipster: Claudette M. Pendleton has been working at home for 14 years in varying roles, including realtor, general transcriber, freelance writer, and essay scorer.

"Invest in a Daily Planner and write down your weekly and daily schedule to stay organized and on top of things. It's a good practice to refer to the planner on a nightly basis to prepare for the next day, and also the first thing in the morning to refresh your memory of all the things you need to accomplish in that day. It is also vital that you write down only the number of tasks that you truly feel you can accomplish in a day, so that you don't become overwhelmed or unorganized."

Tipster: Eddy Salomon (WorkAtHomeNoScams.com) has been working from home part-time for more than a decade performing a variety of jobs, including customer service, data entry, and blogging.

"As a blogger/Webmaster, I would prefer to focus on content and providing value to my users. But I found that I was also doing tech support, marketing, SEO [search engine optimization], customer service, and a whole bunch of other tasks that weren't really adding the value I wanted. So I decided to fire myself from various tasks.

"I listed all the things I did that took me away from providing content and value. I then outsourced these tasks to virtual assistants, programmers, designers, etc. This increased my productivity and the quality of my work because I wasn't running myself ragged anymore.

"In hindsight, it was great that I was the jack of all trades because I was able to hire the most qualified people to outsource the various tasks to. It also helped me determine the fair market value of these services, since you can easily lose your shirt if you haven't walked in those various shoes."

Tipster: Karen Huber has been working from home for three and a half years performing a variety of jobs, including customer service, data entry, medical transcription, and writing.

"Do the most important tasks first for the job. Treat it like a 'real job' where you get up, go to work, shut the door to the office (and lock it if needed), take short breaks, and watch the clock!"

Tipster: Kathy Grosskurth has been working from home "off and on" since 2005 doing short-term project-related work, bookkeeping, and administrative work.

"I think creating separate e-mail accounts for work-related stuff and personal stuff is a must. That way, work can be compartmentalized as work and is easy to avoid during times when work isn't the focus."

Tipster: Janet I. Farley, EdM (janetfarley.com) has been working at home since 2007 as a consultant and writer.

"Call it a day one hour before your official quitting time and use that hour to decompress, appreciate your day's work, and plan for the next day's agenda.

"Also, keep a world time clock/time zone converter on your bookmarks bar. It comes in handy when you live on one side of the world and the person you want to speak to lives on the other."

Saving money

Tipster: Madonna Zimmerman (mgmpartners.com) has been working from home for six years as a Website developer, graphic designer, and copywriter.

"Even those who have a well established business rarely have a 'marketing budget,' which makes it absolutely necessary to take advantage of every possible networking opportunity. Be creative. If none present themselves, create them yourself!"

Tipster: Jane Dohrmann has been working from home "on and off" for four years doing administrative work, desktop publishing, writing, and general transcription.

"This tip is especially for those new people just getting ready to work from home. Don't go into debt to furnish and/or supply your office. Get the basics—even use a desk you already have, for now. Once you get established and start bringing home some money, then worry about it. Save those receipts...they may be a tax deduction!"

Managing children, spouses, pets, and others who share your home

Tipster: Claudette M. Pendleton has been working at home for 14 years in varying roles, including realtor, general transcriber, freelance writer, and essay scorer.

"I have three children and I mainly work from home while they are in school. However, if I need to work while my children are home, I make it clear to them that I will be on important phone calls and should not be disturbed except for an emergency. Also, when I am in my home office, the door is locked to avoid unexpected interruptions and outbursts while I am on the phone. My children are already informed beforehand that if my door is locked, Mom is more than likely still working and should not be disturbed except for emergencies."

Tipster: Karen Huber has been working from home for three and a half years performing a variety of jobs, including customer service, data entry, medical transcription, and writing.

"Try to schedule when others are out of the house, and/or put your office in a quiet place. If needed, shut the office door and lock it. Make sure your kids have someone to watch them while you are working, just as if you were working outside the home."

Combating isolation

Tipster: Claudette M. Pendleton has been working at home for 14 years in varying roles, including realtor, general transcriber, freelance writer, and essay scorer.

"Because I work from home alone, I do sometimes feel lonely and isolated. Nevertheless, I love working from home and I do not desire to ever go back to the rat race. Therefore, to combat the feeling of isolation, during my lunch hour I jump in my car and head to the mall or meet a friend for lunch, or just go for a walk at my neighborhood park. This always helps me, and afterwards I come back feeling refreshed and can finish my work with a better outlook."

Tipster: Eddy Salomon (WorkAtHomeNoScams.com) has been working from home part-time for more than a decade performing a variety of jobs, including customer service, data entry, and blogging.

"When I started working at home full-time, eventually the novelty wore off and I started feeling isolated. So I started making lunch plans with people who still worked outside their home. I felt less isolated from the world and it also reinforced why I loved the freedom of working from home.

"I've also become very active on Twitter.com and Facebook.com. Twitter is like a worldwide water cooler where I can keep up to date on the world, joke with friends, network, and gossip. It almost feels like being in an office filled with different personalities again. Except now, I can shut them off at any time."

Tipster: Kathy Grosskurth has been working from home "off and on" since 2005 doing short-term project-related work, bookkeeping, and administrative work.

"Break up your days; do some volunteer work; have lunch with friends, colleagues, and others periodically so you can be around people."

Tipster: Debbie M. has been working from home since the early 1980s, when she made survey calls, and is now doing research work.

"I combat isolation by going on some of the work-at-home message boards. Some are more businesslike with little personal chat, others are more 'chatty' and have forums for non-business or personal conversations as well."

Making the most of a small office space

Tipster: Claudette M. Pendleton has been working at home for 14 years in varying roles, including realtor, general transcriber, freelance writer, and essay scorer.

"I have a small office space and make the most of it by keeping it clean, organized, and neat. I clean my desk daily, and on Friday I do a complete cleaning to keep things organized and prepared for the upcoming week. I find that when I keep my desk and files organized, I work so much more effectively. As far as saving money on my home office, I only purchase items as I need them for various work assignments."

Maintaining a great rapport with bosses, clients, and colleagues

Tipster: Janet I. Farley, EdM (janetfarley.com), has been working at home since 2007 as a consultant and writer.

"Treat your 'bosses' the way you want to be treated in return."

———◆———

Tipster: Claudette M. Pendleton has been working at home for 14 years in varying roles, including realtor, general transcriber, freelance writer, and essay scorer.

"I believe the way to maintain a great rapport with bosses and clients is to be kind, and to be someone whom they can trust and rely upon. It's also important to be responsible when working on assignments. If you encounter problems, be honest and let them know as soon as possible, so the problem can be resolved quickly. This practice will prevent the company from losing valuable time and money. When your bosses and clients see that they can trust you, a great rapport will be established."

———◆———

Tipster: Madonna Zimmerman (mgmpartners.com) has been working from home for six years as a Website developer, graphic designer, and copywriter.

"Your image of yourself will be projected to prospective clients in e-mail and telephone communications, so make sure you're not still in pajamas with 'bed head' when you start your day.

"The most important tip is also the most difficult. Maintaining a friendly tone in your communications with clients is easy when the client is everything you want them to be. However, it's much more difficult when the client is one you wish you had never landed! It's important to remember that, while this client may be one you're willing to sacrifice, all those who hear about your business through that person may turn out to be valuable clients, too."

Tipster: Eddy Salomon (WorkAtHomeNoScams.com) has been working from home part-time for more than a decade performing a variety of jobs, including customer service, data entry, and blogging.

"I've come to rely on screen capture software like Jing (jingproject .com) or Camtasia to communicate complicated feedback to my designers or virtual assistant. In the past, I would write a long e-mail. But that would end up causing a trail of back-and-forth e-mails. It was just inefficient. But with the screen capture videos it was literally like having that person look over my shoulder as I trained them or explained a complicated problem. I couldn't imagine life without it now. I can focus more on my site instead of back-and-forth e-mails."

Tipster: Kathy Grosskurth has been working from home "off and on" since 2005 doing short-term project-related work, bookkeeping, and administrative work.

"E-mail communications are very important. Providing your superiors a weekly recap of what you have been working on is a good idea, especially if you don't have face time with your supervisors every day. Phone contact can be important, but I think if most communication can be handled by e-mail, that would be fine. But there may be some supervisors who value the phone over e-mail, so you have to be in tune with that and adapt to their needs."

Tipster: Jane Dohrmann has been working from home "on and off" for four years doing administrative work, desktop publishing, writing, and general transcription.

"The best way to keep everything running smoothly and effectively with both bosses and clients is to think of these few things:

◆ Timeliness—If you are to 'start' work at a certain time, start at that time; if you promised a client that you would meet a deadline, then be sure and meet it. These people are counting on you.

◆ Communication—Convey information to your bosses and/or your clients exactly as they request. If they want detailed messages, be sure and provide them; if a client wants research done on a specific topic, be sure it's in the format and detail requested.

◆ Integrity—Honesty is always the best policy. Keep your bosses and clients informed. Everyone wants to know what's going on, be it with their work or the project that you are completing for them."

Making technology work for you

Tipster: Iya Onifa Karade (fonspiritualcenter.org) has worked from home for 12 years as the owner and operator of a metaphysical school.

"Always have a backup plan in case your computer fails! Having two up-to-date computers, one desktop and one laptop, can be a lifesaver if one fails and you are operating your home business on a budget!"

Tipster: Jane Dohrmann has been working from home "on and off" for four years doing administrative work, desktop publishing, writing, and general transcription.

"I want to tell everyone something NOT to do. Don't rely completely on any type of instant messaging. So much information shouldn't be sent over IM. At least with e-mail, you can use encryption resources to ensure more security."

Caring for your most important job asset: you!

Tipster: Madonna Zimmerman (mgmpartners.com) has been working from home for six years as a Website developer, graphic designer, and copywriter.

"It's easy to be so motivated or so into a project that you forget to eat lunch or take breaks, but both are important to avoid burnout."

Tipster: Jane Dohrmann has been working from home "on and off" for four years doing administrative work, desktop publishing, writing, and general transcription.

"I don't have children at home, but I do have cats. At one time I had three of them, and when I needed a break from my desk, that was where I would go to get refreshed and rewarded. The wonderful thing about this is that we, as humans, need time to recuperate and recover from stress (demanding schedules, production typing, etc.), and it's proven that animals can be extremely soothing. Besides, there's nothing like 'unconditional love' for refreshment!"

Authors' note: Chris has two cats (Cheese and Nero), and Mike has a cat (Lilly) and a dog (Primo), and we agree completely with Jane regarding the power of "thera-pet sessions" in the home office.

Tipster: Janet I. Farley, EdM (janetfarley.com) has been working at home since 2007 as a consultant and writer.

"Keep your sense of humor. Every day will not go the highly successful way you imagined it would before you took the leap to work from home. Look for the almost-missed opportunities in those speed bumps of life."

Conclusion

We hope we've provided the answers to most if not all of your questions about how to find home-based jobs and projects, and working from home. (For a handy reference to all the Websites mentioned throughout the book, please see the Appendix.)

For more resources, come visit us at RatRaceRebellion.com, and we wish you every success in your home-based career.

—◆—

Websites Mentioned in this Book

If, as we have, you've ever flipped madly through the pages of a book looking for "that Website" you read about, this section's for you!

Here you'll find a chapter-by-chapter recap of every Website we mentioned.

Introduction

ratracerebellion.com   military.com

Chapter 2: Are You Ready to Work at Home?

mindtools.com   netforbeginners.about.com

Chapter 3: Convincing Your Boss to Let You Work From Home

ratracerebellion.com   ivc.ca

telcoa.org   workingfromanywhere.org

teleworkexchange.com

commuterchallenge.org

euro-telework.org

telework.gov

telecommutect.com

networkworld.com

jala.com

Chapter 4: Developing Your "BS" (Big Scam) Radar

ratracerebellion.com

workplacelikehome.com

complaintsboard.com

ivetriedthat.com

ic3.gov

naag.org

irs.gov

wahm.com

scam.com

ripoffreport.com

bbb.org

ftc.gov

Chapter 5: Good and Bad Work-at-Home Job Search Terms

google.com

google.com/alerts

bing.com

Chapter 6: Jobs by Type and Where to Find Them

Accounting and financial

accountantsinc.com

bookminders.com

clicknwork.com

osibusinessservices.com

balanceyourbooks.com

chmbsolutions.com

firstdata.com

vtaudit.com

Administrative, clerical, and data entry

axiondata.com

diondatasolutions.net

capitaltyping.com

expedict.co.uk

keyforcash.com

officeteam.com

mulberrystudio.com

teamdoubleclick.com

Adult texter/phone actress

1800delilah.com

madamay.com

phoneactress.com

sexyjobline.com

textilicious.com

blvdent.com

papillonagency.com

phoneentertainers.com

text121chat.com

Appointment setting and sales

accuconference.com

bluezebraappointmentsetting.com

extendedpresence.com

telereachjobs.com

callcenteroptions.com

cruise.com

grindstone.com

telexpertise.com

Artistic

3dtour.com

avantipress.com

dragonpencil.com

metaphorstudio.com

victoryprd.com

artdeadlineslist.com

thebradfordgroup.com

tradeleanintree.com

oatmealstudios.com

Call center and customer service

1800flowers.com

alpineaccess.com

callcenteroptions.com

cloud10corp.com

hrccjobs.com

liveops.com

sutherlandathome.com

westathome.com

acddirect.com

arise.com

associatedorderprocessors.com

convergysworkathome.com

hsn.com

newhomebasedccr.com

vipdesk.com

Concierge

officedetails.com

vipdesk.com

Consultants and subject matter experts

beaguide.about.com/topics.htm

brainmass.com

clarityconsultants.com

hireminds.com

dissertationadvisors.com

Courthouse researchers

accuratebackground.com

abcheck.com

work4jbs.com

judgemathistv.warnerbros.com

sunlarkresearch.com

Education, teaching, and tutoring

admissionsconsultants.com

berlitz.com

chronicle.com/jobs

connectionsacademy.com

educate-online-tutoring.com

ets.org

eduwizards.com

idapted.com

nimblemind.com

nrgbridge.com

pearsonedmeasurement.com

smarthinking.com

tutor.com

Healthcare

docond.com

fonemed.com

imagingoncall.net

mckesson.com

medzilla.com

hmspermedion.com

careers.unitedhealthgroup.com

virtualrad.net

Human resources

enidchesterfield.com

ere.net

resumeedge.com

Legal

counseloncall.com	epdine.com
e-typist.com	hirecounsel.com
micromashbar.com	

Medical transcription

accuscribe.net	amphionmedical.com
appliedmedicalservices.com	ascendhealthcare.com
execuscribe.com	mtjobs.com
precysesolutions.com	probitymt.com
softscript.com	spheris.com

Merchandising

actionlink.com	aysm.com
hallmark.com	thehersheycompany.com
narms.com	nis-retail.com
rmservicing.com	sparinc.com

Nonprofit

idealist.org	nonprofitoyster.com
philanthropynw.org	reliefweb.int

Notary (mobile)

24-7nnn.com	americantitleinc.com
bancserv.net	documentsigners.com
notariestoyou.com	superiornotary.com

Technical and Web

accoladesupport.com	ancientgeek.com
arise.com	artlogic.com
authenticjobs.com	computerjobs.com
devbistro.com	dice.com

firstbeatmedia.com

freshwebjobs.com

justtechjobs.com

krop.com

mysql.com

Transcription (non-medical)

accutranglobal.com

htsteno.com

fantastictranscripts.com

emediamillworks.com

mountainwestprocessing.com

nettranscripts.com

thepurpleshark.com

speak-write.com

tigerfish.com

typewp.com

ubiqus.com

Translation and linguistic

butlerhill.com

ctslanguagelink.com

idapted.com

languageline.com

linguistlist.org

lionbridge.com

applicants.rosettastone.com

telelanguage.com

translatorscafe.com

ubiqus.com

Writing, editing, and proofreading

associatedcontent.com

journalism.berkeley.edu

freelancewriting.com

helium.com

journalismjobs.com

jobs.copyeditor.com

placesforwriters.com

proofreadnow.com

sunoasis.com

writersweekly.com

Geographically specific hirers

1800contacts.com

affina.com

aacareers.com

jobs.apple.com

asurionforceathome.com

calldesk.com

csr-net.com

gecallcentercareers.com

hrccjobs.com

infocision.com

jetblue.com

palmcoastdata.com

questdiagnostics.com

micahtek.com

pmresearch.com

telcarecorp.com

Chapter 7: Finding Work-at-Home Jobs on the "Big" Job Boards

monster.com

hotjobs.com

crazedlist.org

bilingualcareer.com

diversityjobs.com

genuinejobs.com

greatinsurancejobs.com

job.com

jobfox.com

jobs4hr.com

latpro.com

prohire.com

talentzoo.com

trovix.com

usajobs.com

careerbuilder.com

craigslist.org

beyond.com

collegegrad.com

efinancialcareers.com

getthejob.com

hound.com

jobcentral.com

jobs.phds.org

jobsinlogistics.com

net-temps.com

retailcareersnow.com

thingamajob.com

tweetmyjobs.com

vault.com

Chapter 8: Finding Home-Based Jobs on Job Aggregator Sites

barefootstudent.com

thejobplanet.com

indeed.com

ask.com

workhound.co.uk

goliathjobs.com

jobcircle.com

simplyhired.com

topusajobs.com

juju.com

Chapter 9: Networking for Jobs, Allies, and Friends

workplacelikehome.com

whydowork.com

cafemom.com

military.com

absolutewrite.com

indeed.com

myspace.com

linkedin.com

hi5.com

orkut.com

plaxo.com

webkinz.com

lindenlab.com

wahm.com

freelancemom.com

ivillage.com

eons.com

vanetworking.com

monster.com

facebook.com

spoke.com

bebo.com

perfspot.com

secondlife.com

maplestory.com

Chapter 10: Virtual and Telework-Friendly Companies

alpineaccess.com

kellyconnect.com

newcorp.com

teamdoubleclick.com

arise.com

liveops.com

sun.com

vipdesk.com

Chapter 11: Freelancing at Home Gig-to-Gig

guru.com

odesk.com

anti9to5guide.com

elance.com

livework.com

ifreelance.com

getafreelancer.com

scriptlance.com

freelanceauction.com

freelancecentral.net

getacoder.com

noagenciesplease.com

rentacoder.com

hotgigs.com

codertribe.com

freelancersoutpost.com

limeexchange.com

trally.com

Chapter 12: Making a Little Money on the Side

Answer questions

aqa.63336.com

chacha.com

kgb.com

bitwine.com

justanswer.com

weegy.com

Take surveys

acop.com

globaltestmarket.com

hcdsurveys.com

lightspeedpanel.com

nielsennetpanel.com

pineconeresearch.com

valuedopinions.com

clearvoicesurveys.com

hbs.edu/cler

i-say.com

mysurvey.com

opinionoutpost.com

surveyspot.com

your2cents.com

Mystery shop

volition.com

aamerch.com

ardentservices.com

checkmarkinc.com

focusonservice.com

intelli-shop.com

ratracerebellion.com

a-closer-look.com

beyondmarketinggroup.com

customerimpactinfo.com

iccds.com

marketviewpoint.com

mysteryguestinc.com

mystery-shoppers.com

premierservice.ca

qualityshopper.org

ms.rentrak.com

restaurant-cops.com

ritterandassociates.com

second-to-none.com

servicealllianceinc.com

spgweb.com

serviceresearch.com

servicesleuth.com

shopperjobs.com

spiesindisguise.com

videoeyes.net

Focus groups

2020research.com

abilitypanel.com

alphabuzzgroup.com

e-focusgroups.com

findfocusgroups.com

hagensinclair.com

Psychics

circleofstars.com

guidinglightpsychics.com

psychicsneeded.com

serenity-snna.com

whispy.com

Writing

451press.com

b5media.com

contentquake.com

families.com

problogger.net

stevepavlina.com

blogsvertise.com

reviewme.com

sponsoredreviews.com

writebite.com

smorty.com

google.com/adsense

affiliate-program.amazon.com

chitika.com

widgetbucks.com

shopzilla.com

azoogleads.com

adbrite.com

cj.com

bidclix.com

Complete tasks

mturk.com

standeejobs.com

quicktate.com

ticketpuller.com

milesofmarketing.com

pixazza.com

shorttask.com

usertesting.com

e-Jurors

ejury.com

onlineverdict.com

jurytest.com

Creative

cafepress.com

printfection.com

artfire.com

dawanda.com

etsy.com

threadless.com

zazzle.com

spreadshirt.com

crowdspring.com

ebay.com

smashingdarling.com

Artificial (virtual)

lindenlab.com

sugarpatch.com

there.com

Chapter 13: Your Telework Resume and Interview

brainbench.com

pdfonline.com

jennwrites.com

freepdfconvert.com

Chapter 14: Tips From the Trenches

workathomenoscams.com

mgmpartners.com

jingproject.com

janetfarley.com

fonspiritualcenter.org

Index

About the Authors

Christine Durst

Credited with founding the virtual assistant industry in 1995, Chris appears regularly on CNN as an Internet fraud expert.

Featured in *Woman's World* magazine as "America's Ultimate Work at Home Expert," Chris has long been one of the foremost authorities on home-based work. Among her many media mentions and appearances are ABC News *20/20*, *Good Morning America*, *Today*, *The Wall Street Journal*, *BusinessWeek*, *Fortune, Consumers Digest*, and nationally syndicated radio programs.

As CEO of virtual-careers training firm Staffcentrix, which she founded with Mike in 1999, Chris co-designs and delivers virtual-career training programs for the U.S. Department of State, Armed Forces, and other clients. Her programs are available at more than 100 embassies, consulates, and military bases internationally.

Chris's first public workshop on home-based careers, sponsored by Microsoft, recently drew more than 500 participants.

Michael Haaren

A former Wall Street attorney, Mike is also a leader and pioneer in the virtual-work field, and coauthor with Chris of *The 2-Second Commute—Join the Exploding Ranks of Freelance Virtual Assistants* (Career Press, 2005), which *Fortune* called "[a] must-read for anyone considering a home-based job."

Mike also writes with Chris the popular work-at-home column for 10M-member Military.com, and serves as the editor of Staffcentrix's 30,000-reader bulletin of home-based jobs.

The president of Staffcentrix, Mike is often in the media, with mentions and appearances including CNN, *BusinessWeek*, *The Washington Post*, *The Wall Street Journal*, *Fortune*, *Inc.*, *Fast Company*, and many more. He co-designs and co-facilitates Staffcentrix's virtual-career training programs for the U.S. Department of State and Armed Forces, and his presentations include the UN, presidential committees, and SBA blue-ribbon roundtables.

Mike co-hosts RatRaceRebellion.com, and writes the Website's popular blog. He graduated *summa cum laude* from Georgetown University and received his law degree from the University of Virginia.